# DEFEAT
## THE DRAMA!

**STRATEGIES TO GET YOUR TEAM
FUELED, FOCUSED AND FIRED UP
FOR GREAT SERVICE**

KIRSTEN E. ROSS, MLIR, SPHR

outskirtspress
DENVER, COLORADO

*If you would like a downloadable version of the Catapult Tasks and forms from this book, please visit FocusForwardCoaching.com and click on the products page to purchase your copy. You can also sign up for our free newsletter.*

Outskirts Press, Inc.
http://www.outskirtspress.com

ISBN: 978-1-4787-2283-0

Outskirts Press and the "OP" logo are trademarks belonging to Outskirts Press, Inc.

PRINTED IN THE UNITED STATES OF AMERICA

# Praise for Kirsten's Work

*"Finding a great coach in the sea of coaches that are out there is a difficult task. Kirsten is one of those great ones. I cannot say enough about the wonderful work she has done with my clients. I get unsolicited rave reviews."*

**Gino Wickman, Author of "Traction: Get A Grip On Your Business" and "Get a Grip: An Entrepreneurial Fable…. Your Journey to Get Real, Get Simple, and Get Results" President at EOS Worldwide and creator of The Entrepreneurial Operating System (EOS)**

---

*"Kirsten is a life changer. I met with Kirsten on the recommendation of a friend last spring and I had no idea at the time how important she would become to my business and my future. Kirsten has the God given ability to connect with people and to help them remove the clutter that blocks them from their potential. Kirsten coached me through one of the most important decisions in my life by opening my mind to new ways of thinking about my company and my job. Kirsten is honest and thoughtful but she is not afraid to challenge you and hold you accountable. I would recommend Kirsten to anyone that is serious about getting empowered and taking control of their future."*

**Andy Goggins, CEO & Owner Northgate**

---

*"Kirsten's unique ability to clearly and quickly identify roadblocks to success and then provide powerful coaching to break down barriers has made a profound difference for McKinley. She is expert at guiding leaders through the most difficult and pervasive challenges. It is a testament to her abilities that she does so with the constant respect and gratitude of her clients, as well. We consider her to be one of our most trusted advisors."*

**Karen Andrews**
**Chief Administrative Officer, McKinley & Assoc., Inc.**

---

*"Kirsten has so many great qualities it is hard to pick a place to start. As a coach, what makes her special is her wisdom. She brings a larger perspective to her client's situations that allow the client to detach from the emotions of what they are going through and to see things as they truly are. This is a rare gift and one she has worked hard to obtain. She is a special person and a great coach."*

**Bob Heinrich**
**Partner at Honigman, Miller, Schwartz & Cohn, LLP**

---

*"Kirsten Ross is an answer to prayer. As the Medical Director of a nonprofit Pediatric Medical and Rehabilitation Program that reaches out to Children with Disabilities and their families, there is a continual need to be not only a great physician, but a great organizational leader. The challenge of casting vision and "leading up" to hospital administrators, philanthropists, and societal leaders can be daunting.*

Kirsten's skill in unveiling the 'best me,' allowing me to 'lead from the platform,' has me believing that I may just be able to take us there."

**Dr. Susan Youngs**

---

"In working with Kirsten I can't begin to tell you the countless number of ways our sessions have impacted my life for the better. I LIVE CONSCIOUSLY NOW. I take control of my decisions, I manage my energy, I set appropriate boundaries and communicate them effectively. I am happier and more focused than I've ever been. Kirsten's strategies really DO work!!!"

**Leslie Lynn Smith,**
**Vice President, Director of Major Transactions &**
**Legal Services**

---

"When I started with Kirsten I wasn't sure how she'd be able to help me and my business. In the first phone call I told her about several issues affecting my office and the morale in it. Over 6 months she helped me gain more confidence and empowered me to lead my employees and business better than ever before. As we changed to a more positive atmosphere the things she said would happen, did. I now have a more positive business and have started to enjoy working in my business again with a new energy and empowered feeling. I would recommend Kirsten and her Drama Free Work Coaching to any employer."

**Dr. Eric Lambert**
**Owner, Discover Chiropractic**

---

*"Kirsten's approach to "Being on the platform", allowed me to always think of being in the center of the audience and taking ownership of my words. There was a lot of junk in the way of being the best manager possible. Clearing out the junk, allowed for myself and others in my team to focus in on the important things such as our operations, customer service, and the big picture of our department for the City of Muscatine."*

**Laura Liegois, Solid Waste Manager,**
**City of Muscatine, IA.**

---

*"Before working with Kirsten, my voice was not heard. As a business owner, I had a difficult time with team compliance and expectations. Through her building workshops and facilitated conversations we were able to come together as a team and I was able to become the team leader and boss I knew I always could be.*

**Dr. Rosemary Batanjski,**
**Owner Complete Care Chiropractic & Be Well in Birmingham**

---

*"Kirsten is a wonderful coach and problem solver. Her ability to drill to the core of the matter is exceptional with excellent suggestions to work through the issues. Sessions with Kirsten will effectively improve all of your abilities to increase your productivity and communication."*

**Paul Redpath,**
**Vice President, TF Barry Co.**

---

*"I had the pleasure to work with Kirsten as my professional coach. She is able to core through the noise down to the key issues and guide you to clear decision-making processes. She is extremely effective in building teams and strong leaders. I hope to continue to know Kirsten for years to come."*

**Karen Walworth,**
**Director of Marketing and Sales**

---

*I would like to acknowledge Kirsten and the difference her coaching has made in my life. She recognized in me false beliefs and bad habits that I had developed that were holding me back in both my personal and professional life. Kirsten listened and provided insights and tools that helped me learn new best practices to hold people accountable, to prioritize and balance my personal and professional responsibilities, to act with intention, to improve my communication skills by taking people along my journey and most importantly the value of having fun. Thank you Kirsten for sharing your gifts with me. You are professional, compassionate, insightful, courageous, and a wonderful role model.*

**Debbie Sorensen,**
**CPA / CFO, High Purity Systems, Inc.**

---

*This book is dedicated to the many clients I have had the privilege of working with. They have allowed me into their world and invited me along their journey. They have been courageous, vulnerable and willing to do what it takes for their businesses, teams and customers. They have engaged in the pursuit of excellence, defeated the drama and achieved.*

*I also dedicate this book to my husband and two sons. We get to share great joy, love, laughter and adventure on a daily basis! I'm so blessed to be on a great journey with you!*

# Table of Contents

Download your companion workbook by visiting the product page at www.FocusForwardCoaching.com to purchase your copy. You can also sign up for your free newsletter.

# Defeat the Drama ~ It is Possible!

*"Anything's possible if you've got enough nerve." ~ J.K. Rowling*

When I start working with a company, the team usually can't even visualize a day of harmony and complete focus on customer care. They cannot imagine a day without drama. Thus, the early stages of my process evokes the usual responses, "It's always been like this," or, "This is just how it has to be. We are too busy," or, "Our industry is unique in these ways." Fill in the blanks.

Nevertheless, it is possible! You can defeat the drama! I have been privileged to be an enthusiastic participant and witness to the positive transformation of many teams, often within just a few months. It requires intentional focus and choosing to do what is necessary. However, it is possible and worth it! The impact on customer service and the resulting improvement in company bottom line are just some of the value this process provides.

Congratulations on taking the first step to defeating the drama and creating a culture that connects with your customers. You are moving in the right direction!

# Leadership Challenge

*"If life didn't give you at least one person not wanting you to succeed then half of us would lose our motivation to climb that cliff in order to prove them wrong." ~ Shannon L. Alder*

This book is for leaders who are ready to defeat the drama and refocus their teams. Leaders who want a business that is both efficient and effective, and a culture that truly connects with their customers.

You've tried every strategy you could think of to get your team fueled and focused. You've worked to streamline and improve processes by implementing new systems, customer service processes, marketing tools and more.

No matter how much money you spend or how promising each improvement seemed, nothing has created lasting change. Your team resists new systems and even modest advancements revert to status quo within weeks.

So far, nothing has created the profitability or the team you need. As a result, you are frustrated, resentful, and resigned. The daily grind and drama in your workplace is zapping the energy and fire you once had for your work. These failed attempts have left you feeling disempowered. You, like many others I've worked with, may feel like giving up.

Imagine what it would be like to instead walk in to work to find a team that is happy to be there, taking initiative, problem solving and working well together; a team ready to take action and excited to provide great service for your customers. That's what a fueled, focused and fired up team achieves. In this book you'll find the tools to fuel your team, create a laser focus to harness the full resources of your business and a fire that generates momentum.

My system can help you create the business and work-life that you desire. I want you to wake up excited to start your day and I want your team to feel the same. You can't run your business alone. This book will give you the tools to defeat the drama and align your team with the needs of your customers.

If you are like many of the leaders I have worked with:

- You are overwhelmed, frustrated or resentful

- You work to exhaustion but feel like you never make any progress

- You are inundated with needless or avoidable customer issues

- Your employees fail to follow-through, no matter how many times you ask

- You feel misunderstood or unheard

- Your processes are falling apart

- You are failing to meet your income goals

- You have forgotten why you pursued your profession in the first place

I wrote this book to help you find your fuel, focus your efforts, and enable your team to fulfill your customers' needs.

## You can Create Real Change Now!
## This Book Will Help You to:

- Find Your Fuel

- Define the Focus for Your Business

- Align the Focus and Energy of Your Team

- Increase Profits

- Consistently Integrate Effective Processes

- Provide Rock-it-out Customer Service

- Delegate Well

- Communicate with Clarity

- Eliminate Frustration, Defensiveness, Resentment, and Anger

- Defeat the Drama!

*Defeating the drama doesn't feel doable? Believe it or not, it is!!*
*And you now have the key to making it happen!*

## Catapult Task: Creating the Vision

If it all begins to feel too hard or overwhelming, like you would rather just limp along where you are because, hey, it's not that bad – take a quiet moment. Stop and think about each of these questions for a few minutes to get yourself on track. Really, experience what it would be like.

**What would it be like to walk into work and have an entire team there for a purpose, not just a paycheck?**

**What would it feel like to have your entire staff energized and fully engaged in helping your customers every moment of every day?**

**What would you feel like if the individual conflicts and drama became overshadowed by the bigger purpose of serving the needs of your customers?**

**What would it feel like to focus the energy of every person on your staff towards one common purpose?**

**What would it look like to reclaim the time and energy lost to workplace drama and conflict?**

**What would it feel like to love your work?**

**Take a moment to write about any additional thoughts:**

One of the deepest innate human needs is to know that our lives count for something greater than ourselves. *Make your business the place where your employees are fulfilling that desire.* This is exactly what fueling, focusing and firing up your team can help you achieve!

- An energized and engaged staff

- Single-minded focus on service

- Fulfillment and fun

## Book Sections

We have many names for the people we serve in business. In my business I use the term client. Others say customer, consumer, patient, or user. The list could go on and on. In this book, to keep things simple I will be using the term customer.

**Section 1: Defeat the Drama: Leaders have the Power**

In the first section, you will focus on identifying and removing your own personal barriers to leadership excellence. You will determine the source of your energy or fuel. We'll also take you through some steps to reclaim and harness your leadership power. In the process, you will become the kind of leader you need to be to achieve your goals.

## Section 2: The 3 E's of Aligning Your Team

In the second section, you will focus on building your team. You will learn how to fuel your team, instill a laser focus on your customers, and enable them to take action with tenacity. You will engage them in your vision. It is an exciting time of sharing! This section will also take you through some of the difficult first steps of evaluating your team members and creating a plan for the future of each individual. These steps will help you remove some of the key barriers to freeing your team to take unbridled action.

## Section 3: Address Your People Problems

In the third section, you will be implementing the tools required to establish harmony and a successful culture. Your challenge will be to take action with employees who are resisting change or are choosing to obstruct progress. The goal is always to help each employee achieve success. However, some will be unwilling or unable to embrace the renewed focus. This section will empower you to take action. I haven't had a client yet who was able to make the transition without some employees creating roadblocks. Addressing your people problems is an unavoidable step to fully defeating the drama.

## Section 4: Defeat the Drama with a Dynamic Team

In this final section you bring it all together. You've worked to fuel, focus and fire up individuals. Now it's time to create a cohesive team. You will identify any barriers to generating a dynamic team that is fully focused on customers.

## How to Use this Book

*"Let me tell you the secret that has led me to my goal: my strength lies solely in my tenacity. ~ Louis Pasteur*

Here are a few tips to use along with the program that will catapult your progress in achieving your business goals and providing great customer service.

## Step One: Read to Learn.

Take in information as a general concept. Do not get ahead of yourself by thinking about everything that is not working or must be changed. Take it one step at a time or you will become overwhelmed and discouraged. This book will help you make step-by-step methodical progress towards your goals.

## Step Two: Focus on You and Your Team.

It does you no good to focus on things outside your business. If you begin to think, "Wow, 'ole so and so sure needs this. They should change this right away," you have stepped outside your area of control.

When your focus turns to others, you miss the opportunity to make change for yourself. Intentionally focus on how the information contained here can positively impact you, your team, and your business. Period.

Too often, we use concern for others as a way to avoid our own shortcomings. So, yes, please do recommend the book to them, but beyond that, drop it and consider your own circumstances. This book will prompt you to do some reality checking that may be difficult at times. When it does, just work to stay in it to get the most out of it for you!

## Step Three: Attach the general concepts to your own work, life, or experiences.

You can achieve a deeper understanding of a new concept by applying it to something in your current work or life. Apply what you learn here to the context of yourself and your business. Use this new information to determine what you are doing well and what needs to be improved. Be honest with yourself. During self-reflection, you will create a list of actions needed to move you, your team, and your business forward.

## Step Four: Take Action!

As you journey down the path of self-discovery or uncover areas in your business that need attention, do not get overwhelmed and quit. Do not say, "There's just too much here. I will do it later." Later may never come. Today is the day.

You've experienced how the inspiration and new ideas from even the best books or conferences are lost if you fail to make an immediate change. Without taking prompt action, the book or notes end up on a shelf, gathering dust.

Do not let that happen here! Instead, take action. Make the commitment to begin the step-by-step methodical process of change that is required. A journey begun whether long or short is better than a journey never started! You will get there.

If you uncover many things that need to change, do not let yourself feel overwhelmed. Instead, break larger goals into smaller tasks. There are exercises throughout the book to help you create a systematic plan to help you do just that.

Remember, you do not climb a mountain all at once. You do it one step at a time.

## Step Five: Do the Catapult Tasks!

The exercises in this book are aptly named, "Catapult Tasks." Completing them will catapult you towards the business you desire; they will help you defeat the drama. You will gain some benefit by reading without catapulting, but it will be less effective. If you take the time to read, take the extra time to catapult! Knowledge you discover in each chapter will build in the next.

You may find it helpful to download the companion workbook located at *FocusForwardCoaching.com* Visit the site and then click on the products page to purchase your copy. You can print the Catapult Tasks (Exercises) on 8 ½ x 11 paper for more writing room. While there sign up for the free newsletter as well.

## Step Six: Commit to Making Intentional Change.

When you see opportunity for improvement in yourself, your team or business, begin the methodical steps required for necessary change. Change will not come overnight. Walking step-by-step through the Catapult Tasks will get you to your goal.

## Step Seven: Stick with it!

Just do it. Keep walking it forward. Don't give up. Don't talk yourself out of it. Don't tell yourself it's good enough the way it is. Something inspired you to purchase the book. Some desire, some hope. Don't squelch it. You can do it! Attack each change with tenacity!

# The Importance of Commitment

*"Unless **commitment** is made, there are only promises and hopes; but no plans." ~ Peter F. Drucker*

Throughout this book, you will see the word commit. Use of this word is intentional. I will ask you to commit rather than to try. As Yoda so brilliantly remarked, "Do or do not…there is no try." I must agree with him. There really are key differences between trying and committing.

We are often unaware of the meaning and power behind the language we use.

My book, *"Playing Life with Purpose,"* has a section on tentative language versus the language of action. Tentative language uses words that water down our message and minimize our power. The language of action uses words that communicate tenacity. **Commitment** communicates tenacity and a pledge towards action. **Try** communicates an attempt at action but tells nothing of to what degree. Try makes no promise of achievement.

To illustrate, hold your left hand up in the air. Now try to put it down. If you put it down, you did not follow the instructions. If you actually put your hand down, you are no longer trying. Trying is not accomplishing what you set out to do. Trying is just a promise to "give it a whirl," "give it a go," "I'll think about it," "I'll make an attempt." Trying says nothing.

Commitment is purposeful. It is a promise to achieve. You feel it. Communicating a commitment becomes a pledge to yourself or someone else. Committing to action is what will catapult you towards your goals. Trying gives no guarantee. This process will require you to commit rather than to try.

Commit for yourself, your team, your customers, your family, your friends. Commit for those out there who could benefit from your work but don't know you yet.

Here is a Catapult Task on commitment. Will you pass it by or will you stop and take a moment to ponder and respond so that this information is cemented?

## Catapult Task: Commit vs. Try

**I see these areas in the past where I have *tried* but not *committed*:**

**I commit to taking the required actions outlined in this book:**

**I will drop the word try from my vocabulary. I commit to commitment.**

**Date & Sign**

# Why You Must Defeat the Drama: A Tale of Two Banks

*"There is only one boss. The customer. And he can fire everyone in the company from the chairman on down, simply by spending his money somewhere else." ~ Sam Walton*

Defeating drama is not just about enjoying work again, that's just an added happy bonus. The real advantage is in the improved productivity and enhanced customer experience you and your team will generate.

My tale of two banks is a true story that illustrates why you must defeat the drama to achieve your business objectives.

I have two boys. When they were babies we opened each of them a savings account in a local credit union. This credit union has a member appreciation program that includes a birthday club for children. Every year my two boys, who share a birthday month, would each get a birthday post card inviting them into the branch for a special gift. The gift was free money in their bank account!

Over the years, taking my boys to the credit union became an important part of their birthday tradition. We'd bring their post cards to the branch and the tellers would make a fuss wishing them a happy birthday with big and welcoming smiles. Then the big highlight, they would get to scoop fake coins out of a fish bowl. They would scoop a handful out and the teller would count the coins. That total went into their back account as actual money.

It was big fun for them! When they were very little they were allowed to scoop with two hands. The total never amounted to more than a few dollars but they loved it and felt very special. They looked forward to it each year. The birthday program was working as intended; creating two loyal customers who would grow up to one day take out car loans and mortgages.

A few years ago, however, I took my two cute little boys to the branch for our celebratory visit. However, everything felt different this time. It was evident from the moment we walked in. As we entered the lobby and crossed to the line of tellers, we were the only customers in the building. We still waited behind the red velvet rope, however, as the sign instructed.

We waited... And we waited... And we waited...

There were plenty of tellers and no visible competition for their time. And yet, we waited.

No one acknowledged our presence as they sat with their heads down.

Finally one of them looked up and begrudgingly said, "I'll help you over here."

My boys walked up to the glass and slid their festive, "happy birthday" post cards under the window with great anticipation. They waited for their big greeting and all the hoopla. This day there would be none of that, however. Instead, with no fanfare and a tone of annoyance the teller said, "I'll come around." She grabbed the fish bowl of fake coins and came out to the lobby to meet them.

Her mood did not change. There was no, 'happy birthday,' no, 'thank you for coming in,' no acknowledgement at all. She was just going through the motions required to complete a chore.

My boys scooped their coins as they always had and she went through the perfunctory task of counting them out and depositing the amounts into their respective accounts. My boys said, "thank you," and received no acknowledgement. The transaction complete, tradition fulfilled, we headed towards the door.

Because my passion is customer care, I am always paying attention to the details of service but I said nothing in the hope that my boys would simply revel in the newfound money.

My boys, however, were more perceptive than I anticipated. Before we even reached the exit they said, "Mom, can we take all of our money out of this bank and put it into Flagstar Bank?"

I wasn't too surprised. The experience had been awful! You see, even two little boys know they deserve better than that.

We did end up taking their money out of that credit union and closing their accounts. I had to agree with their sentiment. Life is too short to do business with people who don't appreciate you. Who wants to feel like an imposition?

At the end of the day, a bank is a bank when it comes to their product and service offerings. The main opportunity for differentiation is in the experience provided while you conduct your transactions.

Flagstar Bank has what they call, 'drop everything service.' When my boys or I walk into the lobby, there is a competition to see who gets to wait on us. They know our names and appreciate our business. They congratulate my boys for making a deposit into their savings account. They tell them, "good job!" It makes them feel proud!

What do I think really happened that day at the credit union? I know that it had nothing to do with my boys! Did I mention how sweet and cute they are? Seriously, though, I think that anyone would have had the same experience. Obviously that branch had some major drama going on. My hypothesis is that one or two of those tellers rarely wait on anyone. I think there was a stand off happening. Those who do wait on customers were pausing to see how long it would take for one of the low performers to call a customer to her window. I think the one who called us over was frustrated and resentful of her co-workers. Unfortunately, that frustration and resentment was directed at, or at least experienced by, my boys instead.

Is this the intent of that post card birthday club? Absolutely not! What leader would spend so much money on printing, stamps, and free money to achieve that kind of outcome? But, the reality is, people and the culture of your business will always be a variable in the success equation. Your team will either help or hinder your efforts to achieve specific results. A post card can't create a customer experience. People will.

Workplace drama takes the focus away from your customers, away from your mission, and away from your business goals. You must defeat the drama to meet your business objectives, whatever they are.

# What is Drama?

*"Our thoughts create our reality – where we put our focus is the direction we tend to go." ~ Peter McWilliams*

We hear people complain about drama at work all the time and I have already used the term in this book a number of times. We have a sense of what it is, but we don't take the time to thoroughly define drama or its cause. So, let me tell you how *I* define drama. I use the term drama very loosely to describe *anything* that shifts an employee's focus away from customers and business mission. Period.

Drama can, thus, take many forms. One obvious example is feuding co-workers who cannot maintain professionalism during work hours. But what about processes that are falling apart? Employees tend to assign this inefficiency to people rather than to the protocol, leading to wasted time spent finger pointing, "They are just trying to make my life difficult," or, "they just don't feel like doing any work."

Or what about the employee who routinely brings life issues to work? They sift through co-workers looking for that sympathetic shoulder to cry on or that special accommodation. Drama!

Drama happens when employees have too much time on their hands and become bored. They drum up excitement unrelated to work to feel that adrenaline rush.

I could go on and on with examples. Here is a list of the most common causes of workplace drama that I see:

**Drama outside the Workplace:** Bringing outside issues in to the workplace. Looking for on-going support or accommodation from co-workers and leaders.

**Process Problems:** Failing processes create frustration and lost productivity as employees create work-arounds or struggle through barriers to completing their work. That creates drama. In addition, humans have a tendency to fault people for process issues. Employees begin to waste time blaming each other. Departments will pit one against another. Sometimes if things escalate it can even lead to sabotage or retaliation as individuals or teams decide others are maliciously seeking to make their work more difficult.

**Down Time:** Too much free time creates opportunity to focus elsewhere, to ponder questions like who said what to whom, who did more work, etc. Opportunity for boredom results in a desire to create excitement artificially.

**Inconsistency:** Inconsistent treatment of employees can lead to drama. Leaders may find it easier to address issues with nicer employees than with defensive employees. Family or dating relationships within the workplace can also lead to inconsistency. Expectations can be higher for better performers than for those who skate by. Whether the inconsistency is real or imagined, it will create drama.

**Inadequate Communication:** In organizations, there can be a lot of talking but not much communication. Inadequate communication leads to drama in many ways. In the absence of data, humans tend to fill in the blanks with negative assumptions. Or perhaps words and body language or tone of voice are inconsistent, leading people to make assumptions. Sometimes there is talking but not enough listening. This creates drama.

**People Problems:** Where there are people issues there will be drama. Some may not have the skills or desire to do well. Top performers end up picking up the slack, which breeds resentment over time.

## Tolerating any of the Above

What is your team there to do? What are they being paid for? Their role is to create a great experience for every customer that walks through your door, calls on the phone, accesses you through the Internet, connects with you on Facebook, or tweets to find an answer.

It doesn't matter how a customer is connecting with you. The gold standard is that every minute of every day during work hours your team is 100% focused on serving your customers.

Drama is the archenemy of great service. The more drama you have in your business, the less focus and energy you'll have for your customers. Period. You must defeat the drama!

## Catapult Task: Where is Drama Interfering?

List as much as you can here. Be specific. It is painful by design. This section will help give you the motivation to keep moving through the steps outlined in this book. Addressing individual issues, challenges and frustrations is more palatable. When you feel that weight of all of it at once it becomes quite a burden.

**Which of the common causes of drama are you experiencing in your workplace?**

**Where is drama winning?**

**Where must you defeat the drama?**

**Drama makes it difficult for us to provide services/products in this way:**

**Drama makes it difficult to provide good follow-through in this way:**

**Drama zaps our ability to provide a remarkable customer experience in this way:**

**Where is Drama zapping your ability to hit your objectives?**

**Where does Drama make customer service less effective?**

**Where is drama making work processes inefficient?**

# SECTION 1

# Leaders have the Power

*"If you do not manage culture, it manages you, and you may not even be aware of the extent to which this is happening."* ~ *Edgar Schein, professor MIT Sloan School of Management*

I cannot tell you the number of times I have heard, "All that people stuff is mamby pamby. I have more important things to do," or, "This is work. It's not supposed to be fun," or, "If they don't like it, there's the door. I'll just get someone else in the position. I don't care," etc and blah, blah, blah.

Defeating the drama and creating a great culture is not just about fun. Yes, a positive culture is more enjoyable, but ultimately, it is about creating a culture that connects with your customers and helps you achieve success. Unless your business is 100% automated, people and their interactions will continue to be a part of your success equation.

Every business has a culture, whether you are aware of it or not. It happens either spontaneously or with intention, depending on your focus. I highly recommend that *you* intentionally create the culture of your business, or your team will. It requires a special culture to connect with your customers. As the leader, you must determine what that unique culture is and create an environment for your team that generates it.

The reality is, regardless of the number of non-leadership employees, the leaders are ultimately responsible for an organization's culture.

If you are experiencing a lot of drama, you are probably thinking, "I would never choose this kind of work culture. How can that be? My team members are the ones showing up late, backstabbing, gossiping, and worrying about who did what. I come in and work hard all day, every day!"

You might be very accurate in that assessment. As a leader you may not be participating in the drama. You might do nothing more than hide from it. But I'm here to tell you that defeating the drama absolutely begins with you!

Now, I am not saying that you are to blame for the drama. What I am saying is that you are the one with the power to defeat the drama. And if you feel that you don't have the power today, that's okay. Follow the steps in this book and you will reclaim your power.

Does this make you feel frustrated or empowered?

I hope it's the latter. If your organization is suffering from drama you have some work to do, but you can defeat it!

You have heard the saying, "Actions speak louder than words." This is especially true here. As a leader, you will mold your business culture through the experiences you create for your team.

In the book, *"The Oz Principle: Getting Results through Individual and Organizational Accountability"* authors Craig Hickman, Tom Smith, and Roger Connors write brilliantly about the leader's unique role in creating a culture. By your title and position you are the most powerful force.

The authors illustrate in a very simple but powerful fashion how a culture is created.

Leaders create:

- Experiences

- Which create beliefs among your employees

- These beliefs drive actions

- And actions create business results, either desirable or undesirable.

Here's a quick example to illustrate the phenomenon.

An employee raises her hand in a team meeting and says she has an idea that will help the company save $500 per month. Her leader's response to this initiative will create a belief in her mind and in those of the other employees in attendance at the meeting.

If the leader responds with excitement and says, "That's great news! Let's implement that right away! Thank you! If anyone else has similar ideas please share them!" the experience will be positive and generate a belief that it is good to be innovative and take initiative. Saving money is valued. This belief will drive actions that are consistent. The result will be a team that seeks out ways to save money and take initiative.

If, on the other hand, the leader responds with anger and says, "Why are you wasting your time on things like that? That is not your responsibility. You need to focus on your job." The belief generated in this scenario is that taking initiative is not valued and can get you in trouble. As a result, each team member will focus only on his or her own job. When they see quality issues or problems that affect customer service or profitability, they will keep their heads down and their mouths shut. And you can figure out how this impacts the organization.

You see, as a leader, you are creating experiences for your employees throughout each day that generate beliefs. Are you intentional about the experiences you are providing? Are the experiences aligned with the stated mission and vision of the organization? Will they generate the results you desire for your business?

What you choose to focus on, ignore, reward, tolerate, celebrate, express anger or frustration over, all send messages to your team about what you value and about what defines success in your organization. And each of these experiences ultimately drive results.

Your team will take action based on the beliefs they hold. The resulting culture either will support you in your efforts or will stand in the way of progress.

If your actions throughout the day are not consistent with the message you give in your annual rah-rah speech to the team, the daily actions win every time.

So, pay close attention to the experiences you are creating for your team throughout each day. Work to make them align with the kind of culture you need to support your mission.

As illustrated in the tale of two banks in the first section of the book, a culture can make or break you. It goes beyond having the right people. Your individual employees really do function like a machine. Many moving parts must work in harmony. One task leads to the next in a sequence. If your team machine is malfunctioning, your business is malfunctioning.

Let's look at some other real life examples of how things can go awry if a culture is not aligned with your business objectives. Even when you've hired a person with the right skills and personality, employees will transform to fit the norm of a team. I have seen similar situations over and over as I begin my work with clients:

- **Example #1:** A new employee is hired for her high energy and up-beat, positive attitude. You feel encouraged that she is exactly what your business or department needs to turn things around. The negativity will be a thing of the past once this little ray of sunshine hits the door.

  Then, three weeks in she is acting exactly like the rest of the team. What happened?

- **Cause:** Her team oriented her to "Here's how things work around here." It is human nature to want to fit in. She was thrown to the wolves and it was sink or swim time.

- **Diagnosis:** You cannot expect a new person in your business to bear the responsibility of transforming an entire culture, especially if you expect that transformation to happen spontaneously. The expectation had not even been communicated to this employee. She was carrying the burden of her leader's hope without knowing. She was also lacking the power of communicated leader support that is absolutely required to enact change in a culture.

Leaders, you are most able to enact change. You can certainly enlist the support of members of your team but it must be done overtly and with a promise to support them as they do battle on your behalf.

- **Example #2:** A new employee is hired to do billing for a large company. She has a great background and comes highly recommended. She works there for 1 ½ years then goes out on leave. Fellow employees take over only to find stacks and stacks of unprocessed paperwork representing tens of thousands of dollars.

- **Cause:** When she first started there was no training to orient her to the specifics of the new organization. She would ask questions but was always met with anger. She was treated as if she were stupid. She had a really good work ethic and wanted to do a good job but she really needed the paycheck and her ego couldn't take all of the criticism. She had been living with severe stress over the mounting backlog of paperwork and did not know what to do.

- **Diagnosis:** The culture did not support training or open communication. Team members were actually hiding issues all over the place trying to avoid the wrath. The culture was so negative that the stress of doing less than standard work was easier to take than the stress of enduring the treatment for owning up to a mistake. Most of the energy was spent on "duck and cover" or "the blame game" rather than on fixing problems or creating excellent customer service.

Now, I am not endorsing the behavior in either scenario. Employees should still always do what is right. However, I *understand* the behavior. Even the best, most well-intentioned people can go into survival mode and act in ways that they would not ordinarily.

A leader has the power to step in and assure that appropriate training is available. Employees cannot.

When you add people, you are doing it to add more heads, arms, and legs into the arsenal. Ideally, these other heads, arms, and legs will be a coordinated extension of you as leader. If your culture is breeding drama, your team is probably not a coordinated extension of you…

When you were young did you ever play that silly arm game? I wish I knew the name. In the game person A stands straight with their arms behind their back while person B stands behind with arms outstretched to become the arms of Person A. If you have children, maybe you have seen them play it. Often person A will recite a poem or sing a song. Person B has to anticipate what they will do next so that they can make the appropriate arm and hand gestures. It rarely works, of course, which always leads to tons of laughter.

This is funny in a child's game but in your business, it is frustrating and inefficient.

You can have all the right people with all the right attitudes, but if the work environment is poor, the team performance will be poor. Bottom line.

The Leaders of Flagstar Bank are only able to create, "drop everything service" by intentionally creating a culture that supports the concept. Hiring, training, rewards, and daily team experiences must align.

I recently visited a store in the mall called, "Buckle." You may have shopped there yourself. The leaders in that organization understand creating a great culture! Their employees were fueled with passion for denim and the coordinating items in that store. You could feel the intentional focus on fun. They know their products, which will work best for your body type, they suggest coordinating items; and even get shoes for the outfit so you could check the hem length. Multiple people made suggestions. They helped each other, and they spoke excitedly to one another about new items they had just gotten in.

Making that happen requires intentional focus. Their hiring and training processes as well as their reward systems and leadership style, all must support that culture. This kind of culture is never an accident.

One of your most important roles as leader is to create a culture that supports your mission and defeats drama. You have the power to do that, if you aren't giving it away to your team. You create experiences daily that help to shape the beliefs of your team; those experiences can be consistent with or can work contrary to what you are trying to achieve.

What kind of culture are you and your leadership team generating? What are you doing to foster more drama and less productivity? What must you change going forward?

To be a great leader you must have vision, integrity, and tenacity. And you, my friend, must be a great leader! Whether you're in a small business or a large organization, your team is looking to you as a guide. You must have a plan and a purpose.

Don't worry! The entire first section of this book is designed to help you become the kind of leader you need to be to defeat the drama and focus your team on your customers.

Now let's get down to business!

# How Do You Defeat the Drama?

*"It is wise to direct your anger towards problems – not people; to focus your energies on answers – not excuses." ~ William Arthur Ward*

Now that we've established that you, as leader, have the power to create a culture free of drama, how do you actually do it?

Let's consider the steps astronauts go through in a shuttle launch. "What does that have to do with my business?" you might ask.

Not a lot. But the laser focus, tenacity, and drive that exists for a team of astronauts during those pivotal moments is what you want to create in your team.

Try to envision for a moment what it must be like during that take off.

That team has a huge mission they must achieve. They know the objectives. Each person is well trained. Each person knows his or her role, and the part it plays in the grander scheme of things. They have sound processes and the equipment they need to be successful.

If even one team member fails to execute with excellence, there are immediate and dire consequences. Think about what's at stake!

Do you think that anyone on that team has the time to focus attention on who did what, who said what to whom, or what politics have been creating frustration? Is anyone talking about whether their spouse is cheating, or their financial troubles?

No, they are 100% focused and engaged on the mission at hand. 100% of their mental capacity is harnessed and focused on the mission.

100% of the human bandwidth is focused on mission.

While I would hazard to guess your business is wildly different from this, you can create the same intensity and laser focus on mission, no matter what kind of service or product you offer.

It begins with generating a team that is fueled, focused, and fired up. And, as illustrated above, that team begins with a leader who can claim the same. You have the power to align your team, create focus, stop tolerating behavior that is inconsistent with the culture you want to create, and defeat the drama.

# Now Defeat the Drama: Get Fueled, Focused and Fired Up

*"To conquer frustration, one must remain intensely focused on the outcome, not the obstacles." ~ T.F. Hodge*

Do you ever wake up in the morning get yourself together and rush out the door only to drive aimlessly in your car all day? No, of course not! But, this is what life looks like when you have tenacity and motivation but no clear road map.

You spend the entire day putting everything you have into something, and you never stop to think about where you are going. It never occurs to you to pick a destination, let alone bring a map.

Running a business without a clear mission and vision is like jumping in the car not knowing where you are going. All the energy, hard work, and strategy in the world will only leave you driving in circles. You must decide where you are going.

When you know your destination and you take the time to get a roadmap, the turns become obvious, forward progress can be measured, and goals are achieved.

I love flying by the seat of my pants while on vacation. It is wonderful to get up with no plan and let the day unfold. You often find great adventure. However, in business, when others are relying on you for direction, you cannot operate like that. It will lead to uncertainty and drama.

In business, you must lead with a blend of clarity for what gives you passion, a clear mission and vision to keep you aligned with that passion, and the self-discipline and tenacity to stay in motion.

To achieve you need a blend of Fuel, Focus *and* Fire.

- **Fuel:** is your passion. It creates the energy and momentum that will keep you moving through all seasons and around obstacles.

- **Focus:** is your mission, your reason for doing business. It provides the road map that tells you which way to go for the journey you are taking. You need this to stay on course and harness the full resources of the business.

- **Fire:** is your accelerator. It's the leadership power that helps you take action and get in motion to make progress. Tenacity requires clarity and confidence, a sure-footedness that comes from knowing that your actions are sound. Certainty breeds momentum and allows for unbridled action.

When you know your destination and have focus, the turns become obvious, you can measure forward progress and achieve your goals.

The fuel of your passion and the focus of your mission will help you create the accelerators or fire you need for success. The combination of fuel and focus will give you the tenacity and self-discipline to catapult your progress, defeat the drama, and create the culture you want. Do not worry if you're unsure at this point. The next steps will help you get there.

How does it sound to be fully charged up and excited about your work, either for the first time or once again?

Let's look at each building block in more detail and then walk through achieving each one.

# Why Fuel is Important

*"Energy and persistence conquer all things." ~ Benjamin Franklin*

I believe that we are all meant to live lives filled with joy and fulfillment; that we have gifts to be used in the service of others. Finding how to use those gifts and live a life of passion is our innate pursuit. I believe that we are fueled by our daily tasks, how we spend our time, the outcomes we are helping to create, and the goals we are helping to achieve.

When you are fueled with passion, you are focused on what is most important to you. You want to go to work everyday because you know you are making a difference. Decisions become easy because you know what you want. Petty distractions are a thing of the past because your purpose is bigger.

Passion is the fuel that pushes you through challenges, both real and imagined, and allows you to see the world as though anything is possible. It is being who you are meant to be and doing what comes naturally. It is like allowing water to gain velocity from its natural flow rather than trying to force it up and over a wall.

When you are attached to your passion, you know you are on the right track, which naturally provides the tenacity needed. You see only that which you seek to achieve! Tenacity drives you through the inevitable challenges.

If you are wishy-washy about your desire to reach a goal because you lack the fire of passion, you will be easily stopped by any challenge. You can tell yourself that, "It doesn't really matter," or, "This must be the sign to work on something different." It's also easier to make excuses, "I just didn't have time for it," or, "Other things just seem more interesting."

Passion tells you that you are on the right track and keeps you moving toward what is possible.

If you do not have passion now, you did at one point. Something drove you through the journey you've traveled and the obstacles you hurdled to be where you are in business. What was your driver then? You had obstacles and challenges, but you did it. What gave you the tenacity to make it happen?

If at this point you are thinking, "wait, I don't think I ever had passion for this work. I think I just ended up here," continue on and let's see if you can find your fuel. If you really can't that is an additional challenge beyond the scope of this book. Contact me and I will help you gain some clarity!

## Catapult Task: Find Your Fuel

If you are without passion, it is time to find the fuel that brought you to leadership in this profession; time to get back to the basics. If you've lost it, you need to find the fuel and ambition you had before it was tainted with the realities of balancing work and family, while dealing with the challenges of your business.

Take the time to sit quietly, close your eyes and visualize. Again, really get into the entire experience so that you feel it, see it, taste it, smell it. Feel again that positive emotion of excitement, awe, appreciation, anticipation, or whatever it was for you.

If you haven't ever found the fuel for your current profession, position or organization, seek it out!

Why do you do what you do? What fuels your desire to go to work? Are you there for just a paycheck or can you get fired up about the work you do or the outcomes you help create?

Once you have it, experience it for a few moments, and then take the time to capture the experience in words here. You will want to look back on this exercise when times get tough. It will help pull you back to your positive and heartfelt experience. This is the reason you do what you do.

**Where were you when you first felt a tug for your profession, industry, leadership or this business?**

**Whom did you first talk to about it?**

**What did you say?**

**How did you feel?**

**What barriers did you identify that you were afraid might stop you?**

**Where did you show tenacity in getting to where you are?**

**What was your big vision then?**

**What did you think it would be like?**

**What was your hope for the future?**

**What did you think when you decided to be in the profession and become a leader - your big ideas - what changes did you plan to make in the world or your community?**

**Take some time to write any additional thoughts:**

Now, visualize the first time you helped a customer or motivated an employee. Or, perhaps there is a time when you helped to create a dramatic difference in someone's life that really stands out. Recall as many details as you can. Even if you are not routinely involved in direct customer care, you have participated in some way in the end result:

**Where were you?**

**What was their first name?**

**What was the issue?**

**What did you do?**

**Who else was there?**

**How did the customer or employee respond?**

**How did friends and family respond?**

**What did you do right after?**

**What did you tell others about the experience?**

**How did you feel?**

**What vision did you create that day for your future in this profession or as a leader?**

**What was your hope for your future?**

*This is why you do what you do, isn't it?*

# Why Focus is Important

*"The sun's energy warms the world. But when you focus it through a magnifying glass it can start a fire. Focus is so powerful!" ~ Alan Pariser*

The his book, *"Be Unreasonable"* Paul Lembert says, "When you are simply following things that seem like good ideas, you are apt to abandon them if you meet obstacles. The idea that once seemed so attractive is not at all enticing when the going gets tough. However, when you and your team are focused on a specific mission, everyone is more motivated to take risks, get in action, and look beyond the obvious."

Why is this true? It's about how our brain is wired.

Without looking, think quickly about how many light fixtures are in the room right now? What color is the car that you are parked next to?

Your brain noticed. But the information was not stored for ready access. You had not trained your brain or requested it to take in that information.

We are bombarded with stimuli twenty-four hours per day, seven days per week. We get stimulus through our eyes, our ears, even our skin. To be efficient our brains register only what we have deemed important or relevant. This information is what I call, "being on your radar screen." Other information is there somewhere but is not stored for easy access.

So, an example would be deciding to buy a specific kind of car. Prior to thinking about this purchase, you probably never really noticed any on the road. However, as soon as you make the decision or even begin to ponder purchasing it, you will see them EVERYWHERE! Did thousands of people spontaneously decide to buy the same car at the same time? NO! You made the car relevant by beginning to think about it. Your decision to make it relevant put the car on your radar screen. You triggered your brain to consider that information important and to store it up front. Bingo! You now notice the car.

When I do my presentation, "Designing Drama Free Work," I often have the participants stop at this point and notice all of the things in the room that were previously NOT on their radar screen. It's a great exercise to help you realize how much you are missing in each moment. Why don't you stop reading for a minute and just do the exercise where you sit.

- Begin to notice the noises that you had just left in the background. Is there air conditioning or heat running? Or maybe you are in a park and there is a din of cricket sounds, frogs, buzzing bees, or birds. Is there traffic noise?

- Look around you at the floor or ground, the bench or chair you are sitting on, the walls or trees, the ceiling or sky. Are there stains, clouds, bugs, paint chips, or flowers that had previously escaped your notice? What pieces of information do you pick up as you intentionally choose to aim your focus in a new direction?

- What are you sitting on? How does your body feel pressed against it? How do your feet feel where they touch the floor or ground? How does your arm feel as it rests on your thigh, the pillow or arm of the chair? How do your feet feel inside your shoes?

All of this information is stimulus that your brain could have readily registered but chose not to according to your current focus.

Now, I am talking about your brain like it is a separate entity. And, in some ways, it is. It does function without our conscious effort in many ways, but we are the ultimate master. We get to control much of the work that our brains do. For instance, we are able to hold our breath for a period, even though our innate functioning will not allow us to hold it until we die.

An example of something outside of our control is that, a primal part of our brain registers danger and fear from novel experiences. It is meant to act as an efficient diagnostic center to help us avoid negative circumstances in our environment. Unfortunately, it is usually calibrated too high and considers anything new and different as a threat. This part of our brain is on autopilot. We cannot turn it off. However, we can control how we react to the thoughts of impending doom and fear. We can stop in our tracks, or we can do some reality checking to bust through that fear and keep going anyway.

Likewise, we can take control of what our brains deem important or relevant so that we are in charge of what data is registered or ignored. This is why creating a focus on a clear mission and vision is so important. Once you have established your succinct purpose, your brain will look for all data relevant to meeting your mission. Any opportunity that will move you towards your mission will come into focus and be stored as relevant. Your brain will hone in on tidbits of information that otherwise could have been missed while non-relevant data is skimmed over.

This is why focusing on your clear mission and vision is so important. Phase 1 is creating it. Phase 2 is keeping your focus there.

Without a mission and vision giving you a road map, you cannot create intentional, laser focus. The target is too large and scattered. Your brain will pick up random opportunities in a scattered pattern. You can't move forward on the straight path that you achieve with a refined focus.

Picture a dartboard. Without a focus on a mission and vision, the entire board is your target. You might pick up a piece of equipment from the lower left side, then hire a team member who meets criteria from the top right, while you create marketing materials designed for top left. They will not be perfectly matched.

On the other hand, with a clear focus, you hone in on the bulls eye alone. Team members, marketing materials, your business environment, customer education, the services you provide, the customer experience you create, and the equipment you purchase are all aligned to hit that one center target. The entire fuel of the business converges. Think of the focused power of water from a fire hose or the Hoover Dam. Harness the power in your business in the same way.

# Define Your Focus

*"The very essence of leadership is that you have to have vision. You can't blow an uncertain trumpet." ~ Theodore M. Hesburgh*

You have found your fuel, or are on your way. Now you must put it to work in your business. As a leader in your organization, your team is looking to you for direction, guidance, and purpose.

It is time to put that vision and passion into words and actions that communicate to others what you would like to accomplish and how your team can be a part of it. Remember, this will become your road map, your core focus.

In this section we will focus on two simple pieces to your core focus:

- What products and services do you provide that set you apart?

- What should it feel like to do business with you?

## Define Your Focus: What Do You Provide?

It is very possible that you already have an official mission and vision statement and that's great! You may want to re-visit those during this section. If you don't, don't worry. In this section you will create a very simple and succinct mission.

The mission statement you develop should get your blood flowing. It should make you want to stand up and fight for your cause. To successfully implement your mission it must be strong enough to keep you motivated. Motivation is only 20% cerebral and 80% emotional. You are relying on emotion to keep this train moving down the tracks.

While the emotion, the fuel, is what drives you to keep at your goals, you must combine that passion with expertise. Emotion alone does not get you very far.

At a minimum, your mission should:

- Communicate the purpose of your organization both internally and to the community.

- Establish a framework for strategic planning and business development

- Include measurable and concrete objectives

- Evoke emotion

- Motivate those involved with your organization to work towards the goals you have established

First let's help you focus on the product or service you offer. Next we'll get specific about the customer experience and how that fits into your success equation.

## Catapult Task: Creating Your Fuel-Inspired Focus

Take a moment to fill in the blanks, either from your current mission statement or starting from scratch. This Catapult Task will help you clarify and verbalize the goals that have you fired-up.

**What unique products and/or services does your business provide for its customers?**


**What unique purpose does it serve to the community and its employees?**


**Your organization was started to fill a void in the marketplace, either to provide something new or to improve upon services already offered through the competition. What void does your organization fill in the marketplace?**


As you look over your answers to the above questions, think of ways to put these pieces together that concisely communicate these points in an emotional way. If you are having difficulty just do a Google search to find some examples from other organizations.

# Define Your Focus: What Should it Feel Like to Do Business with You?

*"I've learned that people will forget what you said, people will forget what you did, but people will never forget how you made them feel." ~ Maya Angelou*

Many of my clients have spent massive quantities of time conducting process improvement initiatives to assure the quality of their products or services but have placed no value on designing the customer experience. Unless you provide an essential product or service with no market competition, the customer experience is an integral ingredient of the focus equation for success.

Let's revisit our tale of two banks. Each institution was providing the same basic service. The key difference was in the feel of doing business. My boys did not like the feeling they had doing business with the credit union. The moral of the story is that interactions are just as important as the services, if not more so. Your customers want to feel appreciated and respected. They want to trust you. Drama got in the way of providing the intended customer experience. Don't let that happen in your business.

Develop a vision for the ultimate customer experience so you can focus on creating that environment.

Here are some of the components of a Great Customer Experience to consider as you create your focus:

- Good follow-through

- Keeping your word; having good integrity

- Timely service and good communication

- Friendly greetings

- An element of empathy when a customer is working through a challenge

- Accuracy in service or product quotes

- Phones answered quickly with a friendly greeting by people empowered to own the issue and to help your customer traverse the inner workings of your organization

- A quick internal response to those speaking on behalf of a customer so they can provide timely, accurate information.

- Every employee must become a champion for your customers.

Create a focus on providing user-friendly channels of communication into your organization: phone, email, Internet, face to face, etc. Then define what should occur during each interaction with a customer. What do you want each touch point or interaction to look and feel like? What do you want the outcomes to be?

Teach your team to acknowledge the customer for the challenge they are working to overcome. Empathy goes a long way towards improving the customer experience in just a few seconds. For instance, if your organization books travel and a customer calls to change vacation plans because they have had an injury, acknowledge the injury before moving on to potential solutions. "I am so sorry you have had an injury! Let's see what we can do to postpone your travel." Small tweak with a huge impact. I recommend putting reminder signs up in front of phones or computer screens so that your team remembers to show empathy before focusing on problem solving.

Make achieving your goals executable by designing processes, responsibilities, tasks, time frames, and assuring that the resources exist to execute well. Treat internal customers as extensions of your external customers. If an employee needs assistance from another department to provide service to your customer, he or she needs to receive timely support. This is internal customer service. You don't want an employee who is helping a customer to get push-back from another member of the team at a pivotal moment.

## Catapult Task: Ultimate Customer Experience

Stop and think for a minute. Really visualize what you'd like your customer experience to be. You can enlist the help of your team on this task if you'd like.

**What are your customers experiencing now?**

**What kind of greeting do customers receive when they come in, call in or email?**

**What do they experience while they are conducting business?**

**What will you do to include empathy or acknowledgement of a customer challenge?**

**How does a transaction end?**


**How do you feel when you experience service like this?**


**What does a customer see when they walk in or visit your website?**


**What does a customer hear in your place of business?**


**What should it feel like for a customer when they walk in the business or call in?**


**What should they see first when they walk in or visit your website?**


**What kind of greeting should a customer receive in person or on the phone? What kind of email response?**


**What kind of energy, service and care should they receive?**


**What does follow up and follow through look like?**

**What kind of expertise can they expect?**


**What should the customer experience be while they are accessing your service(s) or product(s)?**


**What will a customer experience if they must return an item or make a complaint about inadequate service? How will it be handled? What should it feel like to them?**


〜


Keep these Catapult Tasks handy. The information here will drive your decisions in the future.


# Why Fire is Important

*"Success isn't a result of spontaneous combustion. You must set yourself on fire." ~ Arnold H. Glasow*


Now that you are fueled and focused, it's time to get fired up. When you are fired up you are confident and can move with tenacity. Nothing stands in your way. There is no fear or uncertainty slowing your progress. Your energy is high and you are ready to take on the world.

You are free to take unbridled action.

Being fired up is also about harnessing your leadership power and benefitting from the momentum it allows you to create. Much of what generates drama is an erosion of that power. To lead with fire you must reclaim your leadership power.

Many of the clients I work with have surrendered their leadership power and are allowing their team members to navigate business strategy instead. It is rarely a conscious choice. It is something that occurs when leaders let fear or uncertainty win.

To lead fully fired up requires reclaiming and harnessing the power associated with your position. Then you can use that energy as an accelerator for the business. We'll walk through some key strategies to help you do this so if you can't envision it right now, no worries, you are on your way!

In this section, you will harness your leadership, and generate enough energy for you to maintain your own fire and energize your team. A down leader can not fire up a team!

# Harness Your Power to Lead with Fire

*"Leadership is the wise use of power. Power is the capacity to translate intention into reality and sustain it." ~ Warren G. Bennis*

What does it take to be a great leader? There are thousands of books on the topic. In this chapter, we will boil it all down to the basics. Great leadership requires making sound decisions and sticking to them. Great leaders communicate in a way that inspires others to join them on the journey. They base decisions on moving the business towards a specific target. Missteps may still occur, but most of the time they are in the ballpark, not all over the road. The next step is to lead your team effectively so that your capacity to do your work increases exponentially. You, your business, and your customers will all benefit!

# Harness Your Leadership Power with Decisiveness

*"Take time to deliberate, but when the time for action has arrived, stop thinking and go in." ~ Napoleon Bonaparte*

Now that you are focused, you should be able to make confident decisions. If actions move you towards your mission they are a go, if they move you away it's a no. Waffling and indecision come when you lack focus.

Allow others to have input in your decisions; but at the end of the day, decisions are yours to make and own. At some point the conversation stops. Once the decision is made, the team follows. No more discussion.

This can be a difficult transition if you've allowed employees to have decision-making responsibility, whether on purpose or by default. They may act out at first, but keep at it and keep communicating that your decisions are final.

Now, keep in mind, we are not working you towards tyrant status. In the end you will still want your team to have some say and a voice on specific topics. This is about capturing power that should have been yours if you have gone too far on the spectrum of consensus style leadership.

I have helped many clients work through this transition. One in particular stands out. This particular client had been leading by consensus for years. But the culture had grown to require too much discussion and not enough action. If not everyone could agree, nothing got done. I helped him to reclaim his power slowly. He would allow some discussion, but would then make the final decision and expected the team to move forward.

The problem was that, based on experience, they still thought it was debate time. Sometimes they overturned his decision and acted based on their own. We realized together that he needed to make one more announcement about expectations. At times, he would allow the team to make the final decision. On certain things, however, his decisions were going to be the final say. Period. No more discussion. No more debate. Just get into action.

He enlisted his supervisor in the strategy as well. Employees would routinely come to her and say, "You know, I think…" and she would say, "I'll talk to the Director about it." That just perpetuated the culture of debate. They came up with a key phrase that meant discussion over and he got his supervisors on board to say, "Well, that is the final decision. We need to get into action."

If this sounds familiar, you may need to follow a similar strategy to take back the reigns and reclaim some lost decision-making power.

I have also worked with many clients where leaders will not make a final decision. Frustration mounts for the team as the same issues are brought up and discussed with no resolution in site. Employees are forced to struggle through the same challenges over and over and waste valuable time explaining or defending the resulting poor outcomes.

# Harness Your Leadership Power
# with Precise Language

*"You can have brilliant ideas, but if you can't get them across,*
*your ideas won't get you anywhere." ~ Lee Iacocca*

Your team cannot read your mind. Be clear and precise with your language so they know where the organization is heading and what you need from them to get there. I once worked with a leader who made it a game of seeing whether his executive team could figure out what he already had in mind for next steps. He somehow got an ego boost from it. He even laughed at them when they got it wrong. On a personal level, he seemed to gain from it, somehow. From a business perspective, not smart. He was allowing his team to make missteps, and waste time and energy, all to get a chuckle. His focus was in the wrong place and his actions created drama.

The goal is to communicate well so your team can execute well. A quick side comment grumbled as you pass in the hall is not optimal communication. Feeding them crumbs to see whether they can figure the rest out or testing their mind reading skills is not what's best for your business.

If you are suffering from a lack of confidence in your leadership, or are uncomfortable holding your team accountable, or think your employees are already too busy so you feel guilty giving them work, you may be using what I call tentative language as a result.

Tentative language is using words that water down your message. It takes away the punch that they otherwise could have and leaves your team feeling unclear.

Examples of words and phrases that create tentative language:

- Sort of

- If you get a chance

- Kind of

- If you can

- Maybe

- Probably

- Don't you think?

- When you get around to it

Your intent may be to soften the request, but the message you end up delivering is that your task is not that important. "When you get the chance," may feel friendly in the moment, but your employee is hearing that they have leeway. They may never get the chance, so that task may go unfinished forever. There is no call to action. Is that really what you want? If not, communicate the expectation more precisely.

Many of my clients have expressed frustration with their team's ability to follow through only to find that the culprit is the leader's use of tentative language. Remove the unnecessary words and they are frustration-free.

# Harness Your Leadership Power with Integrity

*"Leadership is a potent combination of strategy and character. But if you must be without one, be without the strategy." ~ Norman Schwarzkopf*

Say what you'll do and then follow through. It rhymes and should become your new mantra! Integrity is about saying what you will do and doing what you say. Another key ingredient is owning it when you do not follow this simple rule.

Often my clients intend to lead with integrity but things get in the way. The good news for you is that we have already covered and done some skill building around the main barriers to living and working with good integrity.

If you have a clear mission and vision, it is much easier to be decisive and hold fast to the commitments you make. Decisions made based on your mission and vision should be easy to keep. You will have the tenacity to follow through. The waffling comes when you lack focus. There are more missteps, more opportunities to change course, and thus increased potential for drama. Focus improves your ability to communicate what you'll do and then follow through.

The tenacity that comes with following your passion with a clear mission and vision will also help you walk your talk. Hurdles, barriers, and challenges will no longer require you to change direction altogether. Over time, your team will learn to trust your words more and more.

Fighting the fear and following through with your team will help you live with integrity as well. Commitments to change direction have probably been squelched because of your inability to hold employees accountable. Over time, as they see that you mean business, they will learn to take your word as law.

If you find you have miscommunicated or made a mistake, communication – communication – communication. Own it and move on. No big deal. Sweeping things under the rug can help in the moment but does nothing to build trust or defeat the drama over the long haul.

# Harness Your Leadership Power With Respect

*"Remember there's no such thing as a small act of kindness.*
*Every act creates a ripple with no logical end." ~ Scott Adams*

I encourage my clients to work from the assumption that their employees want to do a good job and deserve respect. However, there are instances when things stand in the way of them working at their best such as, processes that are not working, indecisive leaders (that's you), and expectations set too low.

I have worked with many companies where the group norm is to whine, complain, and place blame on others, a source of great drama. Usually there is at least one employee who fits right in to this environment and probably needs to go; but often it is the group norm that has sucked people in and caused them to behave in ways they normally wouldn't.

Or, rock stars have become frustrated, overwhelmed, resigned, and just don't care any longer. That is frustrating as a leader, I get it.

None of these instances, however, justifies treating people with a lack of respect.

It is up to you, as leader, to create the environment that supports your team working to their potential and to treat them with the respect they deserve.

If you have become frustrated and are acting out by yelling, screaming, throwing temper tantrums or, worse, verbally abusing your team, this is not leadership! And it is NOT lending itself to an environment free of drama for your customers.

Stop!

As the leader, you are the role model for how team members will treat each other. Showing respect requires good tone of voice, volume, body language, and words.

Trust your team to do a good job and make sure they have the tools to do it. We will be covering this more in later chapters, so don't worry about all of this now. Just know that leading with respect is the bar that I'm setting for you regardless of circumstance. Throwing a temper tantrum at your team is not an appropriate response.

The consequence of poor behavior is a professional response in which you reiterate expectations and ask the employee to correct their behavior or encounter discipline or loss of job. Even the employees who are on their way out deserve respect. There's no need for yelling. Walk them calmly through the discipline process as you firmly stick to your expectations and then release them to work elsewhere. Let them leave with their dignity.

# Harness Your Leadership Power with Courage

*"Leadership is the challenge to be something*
*more than average." ~ Jim Rohn*

To harness your leadership power with courage requires us to work on your mindset. You have the right and the duty to lead. You must be empowered. Often, the leaders I work with feel like they cannot get employees to do what they need them to do. They hide, end up doing everything themselves to make sure it's done right, and feel resentful and overwhelmed. Eventually they explode and take their frustration out on their team. But, without consistent follow-through or consequences, the explosion creates no change. The team just waits for the episode to be over and goes on, business as usual. It becomes nothing more than a cycle.

Sometimes there is no explosion. A leader will hold all of the resentment in and feel worse and worse. Health issues crop up; they become distant in their business and at home. The frustration, and resentment build and build and they become disempowered. We need to change that now. None of the work you've done can create change unless you get this concept.

*It does not have to be this way!*

Your team members are an extension of you. They help create your customers' perception of your business. Are they doing a good job or not? If you are tolerating less than what you deserve – why? Stop!! Now!!!

This is a time to bust through your fear and act with courage. To defeat the drama and move the mission forward you must be ready to go to the mat for the business. Ideally, as you begin to truly lead and align your team with your mission, they will rise to the occasion. They will feel inspired and realize it is a privilege to work for you, and that to continue to do so they must follow the new rules and conform to the new culture. But, they might not. They may continue in their current patterns focusing on themselves and the interpersonal dramas they create.

Will your team change or will they continue with their current drama-filled behaviors? This is the big "what if?" It is often the fear of this "what if?" that stops my clients.

Empowered leadership requires that you move through your fears.

Does this sound familiar? "If I lead differently, they might not follow. What if they don't follow? I might need to fire them and I can't do that. So, I will just keep things as they are. We are getting by. Things are fine the way they are."

I am telling you, it is not fine! Drama is limiting your ability to achieve. And, the problem is, this fear is making you give away your power to your team. If you are not willing to go to the mat, if you are not willing to do what it takes to defeat the drama and create the business you desire, you are bobbing and weaving to your team's whim. They are in charge of your workplace culture and they are setting the direction for your business. Where is their focus now? Is it on your customers or on themselves? Is time and energy spent on interpersonal drama rather than on great experiences for your customers? Is this what you want?

The truth about fear is that avoidance does not make it go away. It just makes it bigger.

I watched this in action with my oldest son. When he was about five years old, he became very afraid of thunderstorms. It got quite bad. He would actually sweat and shake and would hide in our basement. Over time, he became more and more afraid. His "what if?" must have been huge! He continued to react to the fear and it got even bigger. He became afraid when it rained, because, if it rained it might thunder. He began hiding in the basement anytime it rained.

Eventually, he became afraid when it was cloudy. If it's cloudy, it might rain. If it rains, it might thunder. He would leave our pool to go inside and hide in the basement. After a while, he became afraid if it was windy. Wind might bring clouds, clouds might bring rain and rain might bring thunder. He would leave the beautiful sunny day and leave his friends to hide in the basement.

I am happy to report that he has busted this one. But it took walking backwards through the levels of fear that he had developed. He learned that it was okay to be in wind, it might NOT bring clouds. Then it was okay to be under clouds. They might NOT bring rain. And so on.

Do you see how the fear is like a blob? It becomes bigger and more consuming the more we accommodate it.

- What fears are lingering in your business and in your life?

- Where is your accommodation of your fear altering the course of your work?

Look back and see the journey that has taken you out of the driver's seat as a leader. Have you just moved to the passenger seat or are you all the way in the trunk? It's a slippery slope when accommodating your fears.

Here are some common fears I come across with my clients when dealing with team issues. It's what ultimately brings them to me. Any sound familiar?

- They might get angry or defensive if I ask them to change.

- They might not like me.

- He might have a nervous breakdown.

- They might not listen.

- They'll just keep doing it the same way anyway.

- She is going through a hard time and might feel worse.

- I can't fire so and so, they are the niece to my long-time customer of 10 years.

- He knows everything about my business.

- I'll have to hire someone new, it will take forever, and they'll be just as bad or worse.

- I'll have to teach someone new. It takes too long.

- She might go work for a competitor and take all of my customers with her.

- He's the only one who knows how to do – fill in the blank.

I am going to hypothesize that you have fear stopping you in this area. I know you do not know all the steps to fix your team issues and defeat the drama yet. It's okay. You will. As you progress, this book will continue to build your knowledge and skills. However, for this chapter I am asking you to explore your fears, bust through them, and move forward. Can you commit to doing that?

You have the power, *all the power*, in your business.

- Will it be easy? Maybe not, but few things worth achieving are.

- Will there be a time of transition? Yes.

- Will there be some negative fall out? Possibly.

- Will the fallout be worse than what you are experiencing day to day now? No!

- Will it be better in the long run? Yes!

Without exception, every client I have worked with who has followed the steps you are about to take has been happier and more successful as a result. And all have found it easier than they imagined. Because, as is often the case, our fearful version of what might be, is far worse than the reality of what is.

Are you ready to take back the power in your business, act with courage, hold your team accountable, and lead?

## Catapult Task: Evaluating My Fears

The problem with fear is, often we focus on avoiding it instead of determining exactly what we are afraid of or how real the threat might be.

**My fear about truly leading my team and holding them accountable is (*be specific*):**

**Reality Check. What is the worst-case scenario?**

**What are the chances of this happening – *REALLY*?!**

**Would it really matter that much if this did happen?**

**I suffer these consequences by allowing these fears to win:**

**My (business, departments, unit, division, team) suffers these consequences by allowing this fear to win:**

**My customers suffer these consequences when I allow my fear to win:**

I commit to taking these steps to diminish this fear and expand my influence. Start big or small, just get moving to expand your life!

What successes have you experienced? Keep track of these until you get good at busting through your fears. They will give you fuel to keep playing larger and larger.

❧

## Catapult Task: Harnessing Your Leadership Power

I am creating these experiences that do not support the culture required to meet my mission:

I see where my waffling decisions or lack of decision-making has caused my team these issues:

I see where my decision-making issues have caused these issues for my customers:

I use these phrases and words that water down my message:

It has this impact on my customers and team when I water down my message:

**I commit to communicating with tenacity and will use these strategies:**

**I fail to show respect for my team in these ways:**

**I commit to using respect in my words and actions in these ways:**

**I lack integrity in these areas:**

**I commit to making sure my words and actions match in these instances:**

**My leadership style is negatively impacting my business in these ways:**

**I commit to creating these experiences for my team so our culture aligns with my mission:**

**I will harness my leadership power in these ways:**

# Harness Your Energy to Lead with Fire

*"Failure is more frequently from want of energy*
*than want of capital." ~ Daniel Webster*

As a leader, you must make a commitment to stay fired up and maintain your energy. Remember, you are creating experiences for your team daily. You set the standard through both your word and actions. You cannot create more time but you can create more energy. And once you have optimized your energy, you can focus it to create your desired outcomes.

Can you think back to a time when you felt hopeless? That feeling that you are just sick and tired of the same old thing when it feels like nothing will ever change. What did that feel like energy-wise?

Now think about how much energy you have when it feels like everything is going your way, when you are joyful and almost feel like skipping, when a smile is plastered on your face and you want to laugh at everything around you. You have much more energy. When your mood is up, you are fired up.

In the book, *"Power V Force"* by Dr. David R. Hawkins, M.D., Ph.D., he shares the findings of a study done on the vibrational energy created by different emotions. They were actually able to substantiate that emotions like anger, disappointment, revenge, jealousy, and fear all have lower vibrations than the higher-level emotions like love, joy, enthusiasm, and hopefulness.

They also conducted some studies where they were able to measure the impact one person with high energy could have on others.

Conversely, the low energy of one individual can impact the energy of others. I'm sure you've experienced this one yourself. You walk into a room where someone is so down and out, they seem to be sucking up any available energy from around them. If you aren't careful, before you know it, you are yawning and feeling low energy too.

To be a great leader, you must harness the power of your energy and protect it.

You have the ability to maintain a high energy level. It is not necessarily something that will happen spontaneously though. Choose to be the person who is fired up and boosts the energy of those around you. Your team needs you to bring the energy up and lead with fire.

Here are some strategies to help boost and maintain your energy for fire.

## Harness the Energy of your Thoughts

*"Thoughts Become Things... Choose The*
*Good Ones!" ~ Mike Dooley*

Did you know that the average person has approximately 70,000 thoughts per day? Are you even aware that you are empowered to choose the kind of thoughts that you will have? Regardless of circumstance, you can choose your thoughts. That means that you have 70,000 chances to choose thoughts that inspire you or thoughts that bring you down. Thoughts impact your mood and mood helps maintain energy.

Here's the road to energy:

- Circumstance – Something happens

- Chosen Thoughts (Story) – You give it meaning by assigning a story about what happened

- Response - Your story generates a response in you

- Emotion – You will have a corresponding emotional response

- Energy Level – Your emotional response determines your energy level.

The stuff that we experience doesn't have meaning until we assign the meaning. Assigning the meaning is what I call telling the story. It's the story that makes a happening emotional. That story will either create positive, empowering emotions or negative, victimizing emotions.

Throughout your day, you continually process your circumstances and the things you tell yourself about those circumstances make up the story of your life. The story you tell yourself in each situation will help to create your response. Your response creates your emotion. Your emotional state is a factor that determines your level of energy.

So, you can't always choose your circumstance but you do get to choose your reaction to your circumstance. In other words, you can control the thoughts that you have about a situation, which will change the emotions you generate.

Now, there is a difference between stuffing emotions and powerful-ly choosing an emotional response. I am not asking you to become an expert emotion stuffer.

Emotions do give us important information. There are times when a negative emotion is warranted and should be there to encourage us to take some action. At other times, however, circumstances are generating unrelated reactions.

Emotions are not fact. We should pay attention to them but they should not drive our entire lives. There are times that the emotions we experience are not even directly related to the current circum-stance. A past hurt may trigger a current response. And at times our capacity to manage a frustrating situation can be greatly diminished when we are tired or hungry.

An employee cutting you off on the way into the staff parking lot during a low stress kind of day might seem humorous. Experience that on the day of your big presentation when you've been up for 3 nights with a toothache and that co-worker may garner an entirely different response if you let it.

Really take a minute to think about this if it is a new concept for you. There are times that it takes weeks for some of my clients to get this one. They are not convinced until they experience the power for themselves. Sometimes they get angry with me as I try to explain that they cannot control their circumstance but they do get to control their reaction to it. They tell me story after story of frustration. I still come back with, "You can't always choose your circumstance but you do get to choose your reaction." Or, I will say, "Anger is not a required response in that situation. It is what you chose."

Once you understand this concept there is no going back. Once you take the blinders off and have this awareness, you are empowered for life. It's a cool one to get! So worth the extra time!

Here's a quick little exercise to try. We won't dub this one a Catapult Task. It's just a food for thought activity.

Think of a situation that you experience that routinely causes you frustration. We'll start with a relatively easy one. Some examples might be a know-it-all neighbor, your spouse saying that same thing again and again, a person at the gym who always hogs the machine, traffic tie-ups on your way to work, an employee who complains about the same thing every day, a mother-in-law.

Picture it. Get the frustrations really going. Feel it. Now, stop and think of all of the other emotions that you could CHOOSE to have about this situation. Take a minute to experience each one:

What if this scenario made you paranoid?
What if it made you sad?
What if it made you calm?
What if it made you laugh? Maybe it's the most hilarious thing you've ever heard!

What other emotions might you feel about it?
What other story might you tell yourself about it?

You have all of these emotions, each of these stories, available to you as an option every time you have this experience.

To walk through and fully get each of these steps may take time, maybe even several weeks. I ask you to commit to working on it

- At a minimum, I request that you begin to consider the possibility that you do have options and you are *choosing* your response. – *Can you do at least this?*

- Once you are able to realize it, do the task again and begin to **know**, take in as fact, that you are choosing your response.

- When you are ready, practice choosing a different response. You don't have to commit to it. Just try it on for size. What does it feel like to find traffic a gift? What does it feel like to know that your mother-in-law's comment is the most hilarious thing you've ever heard?

Now that you know that you have the power to choose your response, choose to think and be in a way that allows you to focus on success. Pay attention to your own energy. You get to tell the story of your life. Why not choose thoughts that keep your energy up?

Also be aware of the energy of others and put a barrier between you and those with low energy. Do not allow those with low energy to pull yours down.

## Harness the Energy of Celebration

*"The more you praise and celebrate your life, the more there is in life to celebrate." ~ Oprah Winfrey*

Putting your focus on celebration is a strategy that will help you increase your energy. So be the kind of leader who looks for reasons to celebrate with your team. There will always be things to work on, goals not yet achieved. I'm not suggesting you turn a blind eye.

But you can't put one hundred percent of your focus there. That just makes for a frustrated leader.

In each moment, there is opportunity to focus on either what is being done well or what is being done wrong. Mistakes and unmet objectives have a tendency to come at us as issues or complaints. To shift your focus to the things done well, you must intentionally seek them out. If not, we can miss them and end up spending all our time fixing issues. This does not boost energy.

Consciously seek out opportunities to celebrate every day. Set a weekly or daily goal that can be celebrated.

And, by celebrate, I don't mean throw a big party with hats, noise-makers, and food and drinks. You can have a one-person celebration sitting at your desk. Just take one minute to stop and think, "Ahhhhh, I am awesome," or, "We made great headway yesterday." Just feel yourself relax and enjoy the accomplishment, the progress, even if it is just for a moment.

That's it. That's a celebration.

Without intentionally choosing to spend time celebrating, it is so easy to get caught in the grind of just doing without realizing the progress made.

Set achievable goals tied to business objectives or customer service standards and then celebrate achieving them. I've had many clients use this technique and it absolutely helps.

# Harness the Energy of Gratitude

*"We can only be said to be alive in those moments when our hearts are conscious of our treasures." ~ Thornton Wilder*

Practicing the art of gratitude is about maintaining a focus on all that you can appreciate. In every moment of every day there are reasons to be grateful. It's as simple as shifting your focus from worry to wonder.

Consider starting a gratitude journal. Write in it first thing in the morning or at night before you go to bed. Or, keep it in your car and jot things down while you are sitting at a light. As you spend your day looking for things to be grateful for, you will find your focus magically shifted. It will become easier and easier to find positive things. Gratitude is a great source of positive energy.

I have had times in my life when outer circumstances were especially stressful. I was really struggling to keep my focus positive. I kept my gratitude journal right next to me all day, writing in it throughout the day or each time I thought of something else for which to be grateful. And it worked. Spending even a portion of a day doing that can shift your focus for a few weeks. For real, it is magical! It really is. Try it!

Still having trouble thinking of things? Here are some ideas:

- Beautiful day

- Rain to water the grass for free

- The transportation that got you to your destination

- Family

- Friends

- Hitting your customer volume goals

- Having great customer flow

- Helping a customer

- Your legs that carried you into the building

- Your hands that help heal

- Your team members

- The food you had for breakfast

- The trees and flowers

- The people who plow snow off the streets

- The teachers in your children's school

- The crossing guard who helps your child stay safe

- The roof over your head

- The bed you slept in last night

- Coffee

- Tea

- Your cell phone

- Internet access

- Your spouse

- Your health

- Your kids

- Heat or air conditioning in your building

## Catapult Task: Harness Your Energy

**I see these tendencies in my thought patterns:**

**I commit to creating stories about my work that create more energy in these areas:**

**I commit to the following to add celebration to my business this week:**

**I set these achievable goals tied to business objectives as targets to hit and celebrate:**

**We will celebrate in these ways:**

**I am grateful for these things right now:**

**I will focus on gratitude daily in these ways:**

# SECTION 2

# The 3 E's of Aligning Your Team

*"One man can be a crucial ingredient on a team, but one man cannot make a team." ~ Kareem Abdul-Jabbar*

Unless you plan to run a tiny business with a very localized mission, you cannot achieve your important goals as a lone ranger. To accomplish great work you must increase your circle of influence. You must focus your time and energy on utilizing your gifts while also allowing others to utilize theirs in support of the business mission. You need the impassioned support of an integrated, efficient team. You need a team empowered to do their jobs and aligned with your business mission; a team equipped with the tools, processes, and resources they need to be successful.

Now that you are fully fueled, focused, and fired up, it is time to take the next steps to generate a fueled, focused and fired up team and defeat the drama. You must be sure that your team, both individually and collectively, is acting as a coordinated and impassioned extension of you. That the activity, energy, and full resources of the business are laser focused towards the business objectives and customer experience that you have defined, and away from drama.

As you move forward in the next chapters, the tasks may get a bit harder. Know that all elements here are important pieces of the puzzle and many build from concepts you have learned in prior chapters. Unfortunately, there is no magic pill that makes this next series of steps smooth. You are entering a time of transition for you and your team. There will be hiccups, missteps, uncertainty, fear, and frustration. Sometimes realizing that these are a normal part of the process is helpful. Keep your eye on the prize: defeating the drama and creating a culture that connects with your customers. Do not let the discomfort of change derail you or your team.

We will travel through the three key ingredients to align your team with the business mission of generating great customer care.

The 3 E's of Alignment are:

- Engage Your Team with Fuel

- Empower Your Team to Act with Focus

- Energize Your Team for Fire

# Engage Your Team with Fuel

*"Leaders touch a heart before they ask*
*for a hand." ~ John C. Maxwell*

You are fueled, focused, and fired up; now let's get your team there! In this section, you will learn the steps required to create an impassioned call to action to share with a team that is empowered and working like a well-oiled machine, aligned with your business mission.

Why do you want an engaged team? This is an important question, as is the case in many instances in this book, starting with the, "why" helps build your motivation for change.

Did you know that in the past, one of the tortures of war was doing physically demanding work for no purpose? Warlords had their prisoners spend entire days moving giant dirt piles from one side of a field to the other, back and forth. Work with no specific outcome, no mission, no vision, and no purpose.

It is not the tough work that is most difficult to bear. It is doing work with no goal to pursue. As humans, we have an innate desire to know that our lives have a purpose greater than ourselves. It is torture to feel like we are living lives like a hamster on a wheel, that all of our work is for nothing. Human beings fueled by passion will move mountains without hesitation. And they will feel good at the end of it, if they have a vision for the outcomes they are helping to create.

Do not let your workplace and the tasks that take place there be like those piles of dirt. Make sure that your employees know the value of what they are doing and why. How does each shovelful help them meet the bigger mission?

Help your team attach every task they do to the bigger mission. You want them to internalize your mission to elevate the importance of even the smallest duty.

As a leader, help your employees find their fuel. Engaged team members feel that they are part of something bigger, something more important than their own personal drama. They feel like a valued member of a team.

It becomes important to come to work everyday and they are given a reason to do the best possible job they can. Not out of fear but out of a desire to achieve outcomes they are excited about.

When others on the team stand in the way, they seek to bring the team back on track rather than participate in any kind of drama. A team that is wired for passion is efficient, hard working, and takes pride in what they accomplish every day.

Passion will motivate your team to great achievements and will focus their energy towards a common goal.

**An Engaged Team**

- Achieves more than non-motivated employees

- Is less likely to leave your organization

- Is loyal

- Has better morale

- Takes fewer days off

- Rises to the challenge

- Gets more done

- Creates bigger outcomes

- HAS LESS TIME FOR DRAMA!!

And it's not just about your team. As I've already illustrated, when customers walk into a business that is driven by a common purpose, they immediately feel the difference. They feel supported and cared for. The team is polite; things move smoothly. And when things don't go smoothly, there is a caring person ready to help, an employee who is fully focused on the customer and who knows they have a team to back their efforts. Customers are able to relax and focus on their own needs because they are in a comfortable, friendly environment where others are truly interested in them.

Negative dynamics, on the other hand, lead to stress, which has serious negative implications for you, your team, your customers, and your business.

Team members that are under damaging levels of stress exhibit the following behaviors and consequences for the organization:

- Carelessness and increased accidents

- Increase in sick days or personal vacation days

- High turnover rates

- Irritability and poor attitude

- Irrational behavior and difficulty with decision making

- Not motivated by work that they would otherwise be drawn to

- Increase in customer complaints

- Damage to the public image of the organization

- Increase in legal liability due to employee negligence

When your team is experiencing high levels of stress because of the work environment, there is a noticeable increase in mistakes and poor decisions. Team members begin to cut corners on issues like product quality and customer care, either intentionally or unintentionally.

The American Institute of Stress estimates that organizational stress and the problems stemming from that stress siphons 20% of a company's payroll. Imagine what you could accomplish by eliminating this stress. You could hire additional team members, invest in new equipment, or update your facility.

Remember, we are all born with an innate desire to know that our lives have a purpose. Sometimes we are not consciously aware of this desire. Some people go through life with the feeling that there must be more. But they never stop to think about why or how they could change their life's direction by changing their perspective or taking some action.

We all have unique gifts that we are given to use in service to others. Those gifts may help others directly or they may be used in support of those who provide the direct impact. All are necessary. All are important.

Many people do not think of themselves, their talents, and their energy as a resource. It is important to do so. When you begin to think that way, you start to become more intentional about where you want to invest your gifts.

When I graduated from Michigan State's Masters Program, I became a highly sought after commodity and was recruited by many large organizations. I decided that I must feel good about the company and the product or service they were providing. I made a conscious choice to turn down interviews with companies not aligned with my values. I felt like I had talents to share and wanted to put my energy where I had passion. I ended up working in a health care setting. I was not directly involved in patient care, which is not my area of strength. But I could help impact the work-life of those who were helping patients, and through them, I would positively impact patients and help heal.

You need to help your team do the same, if they haven't already. Even if they aren't directly involved with your customers, they still have an important role to play in allowing you to do what you do well. Help them identify their individual gifts, provide them with the resources to be successful, and attach them to your mission.

A second human truth is that we all have fear. We each have a section in our brain that functions to keep us safe. That part of the brain must work efficiently, so it makes snap judgments. Anything determined to be new or unfamiliar is quickly identified as dangerous and something to be feared. As a result, we must learn to work around our fears constantly. No one is without fear. The outcomes in our lives are based on what we do with that fear. Some people let fear stop them in their tracks while others bust right through with little more than a glance.

You want your vision to be more compelling than your employee's fears. They will have these fears and more:

- Fear of failure

- Fear it won't work

- Fear of the unknown

- Fear of looking silly

- Fear of not being good enough

- Fear of what others might think

Give your team a great mission to work towards that will inspire them to bust through their fears and hurdle any barriers with ease. Give them the gift of tenacity with the energy of your vision.

We have covered the *"why,"* to give you the motivation, now let's talk about *how* to get your team fired up!

# Engage Your Team: Share Your Mission

*"A leader's role is to raise people's aspirations for what they can become and to release their energies so they will try to get there." ~ David Gergen*

It's time to share your mission. You can use the scaled down, basic version of, "here's what we do and how we do it," or dig in to the full mission and vision. Regardless of which you choose, you want every employee to see it, read it, memorize it, and internalize it. Each member of your team must feel the importance of the business mission. It isn't enough that they see it every day or even that they can recite it. They must feel passionate themselves about your goals. They will develop that passion by first seeing it in you. You are their leader; they look to you for cues about what is important and what is not. You need to share your mission statement with them in a way that conveys how meaningful it is to you, as their leader.

All of us want to be part of something bigger than ourselves; it is human nature. Make this the opportunity your team has been looking for. When they feel your passion and know that they are part of your mission, they will want to come to work every day. Give them a reason to be better and to work harder. Give them a reason to come to work every day beyond simply receiving a paycheck.

## Share Your Mission: Help Them Feel It

You must share your mission with emotion. Passion is no more than 20% cerebral and 80% emotional. You cannot think your way to full passion. You cannot just send an email or hand everyone a piece of paper in a meeting. They need to *FEEL* your mission. Let your fuel create contagious enthusiasm. Authentically share. Let them hear the excitement in your voice!

Begin at the beginning. Why did you enter this industry or profession? When did you first discover this need in the world or birth this business idea? Where were you? What did you experience as you felt that undeniable tug in your chest? What did you think? What will it feel like to provide this product or service? Share some information from your Catapult Task *"Find Your Fuel."*

Be vulnerable and authentic with your team. Just tell it like it is, from the heart. That is what creates human connection. That energy will be transferred to your team.

## Share Your Mission: Help Them See It

Post your mission for all to see. You should have it hanging visibly in your office, in the break room, in the hall. Put it at the top of your written communications, have it in a frame during your team meetings. Keep your mission at the forefront of everyone's mind. Make sure that your employees know why you are in business and how it should feel for your customers to access your products or services. Keep everyone focused on the important difference you are making in the world.

## Share Your Mission: Help Them Join It

Each team member is a valuable resource and each needs to begin to see themselves that way. They have been given gifts to be used in the service of others. Your business is where they will have the opportunity to fulfill their purpose.

Help your team realize that they are important resources. You cannot do it without them. Create a mantra in your office, "We all help provide great service." Depending on the size of your business, you may have team members not directly involved in customer care. Left to their own assumptions, they may feel like their work is not as important. It is possible you are cementing this belief. Many of my clients celebrate the achievements of those participating in sales but fail to recognize the administrative staff who helped behind the scenes. Each team member needs to realize that he or she is an integral part of fulfilling the business mission whether they have direct customer contact or not.

Take the time to brainstorm about how each task helps fulfill the bigger mission. Ask your employees to think about the work they do and how they could each step up their game to help you accomplish your goals faster.

When I first started working on the presentation that this book is based on, I titled it, "Even Cleaning Toilets Can Be Fun." That title didn't stick, for obvious reasons, but I don't want to lose the importance of the concept. If you can attach even the smallest, most seemingly insignificant task, to the huge impact you are making, that task is elevated in importance. The focused energy, the mindset, and the attention to detail, are all heightened to match.

A housekeeper in a business setting inspired that title. Years ago, I worked in Human Resources for Cottage Hospital in Grosse Pointe, Michigan. This particular housekeeper was always so friendly and enthusiastic. I knew her job was tough and certain aspects of it, particularly in a hospital, could be quite disgusting. So, one day I asked her how she did it, how she stayed so upbeat and seemingly unaffected by the work she was doing. She said, "I don't really think about the actual work. I focus on the patients I am helping. I have empathy for them. I know that when a patient makes a particularly big mess (I won't get graphic about what she actually said here) I know that the patient must be feeling really, really bad. I focus on them and doing what I can to help them feel better. That way I never mind the work that I am doing, no matter what."

See, she was not technically involved with patient care but she chose to see her work for how it could positively impact the patients. From there, she was able to maintain her enthusiasm for what could otherwise be a pretty thankless job.

Every task in your business can be similarly attached to your bigger mission. Help your team begin to reframe their duties into mission centered job statements. Whether their official title is Accountant, Purchase Representative, Warehouse Supervisor, or Customer Service Representative, begin to speak about the positions and tasks in a new way.

Let's look at some examples of what a difference it can make when you elevate each job and task and speak about it in terms of the difference it can make towards meeting your mission.

**Receptionist:**

**Current:** I answer phones, schedule appointments, and have customers fill out paperwork

**Mission-Centered Job Statement:** I create a welcoming environment for people seeking help. I make sure they are scheduled for their appointments with us so they receive the help they require. I route calls to the appropriate person so our customers' needs can be met efficiently.

**Biller**

**Current:** I enter all billable hours and materials.

**Mission-Centered Job Statement:** I work to establish great relationships with our customers' accounts payable representatives so we receive appropriate pay with minimal delay for the work that we do. This keeps our doors open so we can continue serving our customers.

**Office Manager**

**Current:** I handle all the problems.

**Mission-Centered Job Statement:** I take the administrative work from the leaders and maintain a smooth running office so our team can serve more customers.

**Janitor**

**Current:** I dust, mop, and clean.

**Mission-Centered Job Statement:** I create an environment that is inviting to our customers and communicates organization and efficiency.

**Massage Therapist**

**Current:** I do massages

**Mission-Centered Job Statement:** I bring comfort to the patients' bodies so they can be more active in pursuing their own life goals.

You get the picture. Have your team begin to attach their tasks to the bigger mission. Encourage them to be creative and have fun with the exercise of creating mission-centered job statements.

We will dive deeper into giving your team opportunities to participate in another section. For now, let's just focus on helping each member of your team see and feel the important role they play in achieving the business mission and providing great service.

## Catapult Task: Sharing the Mission

**I will include the mission and vision in our meetings in these ways:**

**I will help my team feel the mission in these ways:**

**I will use these strategies to keep the mission top of mind for our team:**

**Mission-Centered Job Statements: Create a mission-centered job statement for each position. Provide each team member the opportunity to re-frame the significance of their job by attaching it to the bigger mission in 1 to 3 sentences.**

# Empower Your Team to Act with Focus

*"The best executive is the one who has sense enough to pick good men to do what he wants done, and self-restraint to keep from meddling with them while they do it." ~ Theodore Roosevelt*

You have fueled your team with your mission and vision. Now it is time to unleash them to do their best work with a clear focus.

Remember, the goal is to increase your circle of influence as a leader. Your team must be a coordinated extension of you with a clear focus on mission, not a puppet on a string. You cannot control each move that every employee makes. Your team cannot be efficient if you are involved in every decision or action. You will become a barrier and this will create drama.

Your employees are fueled for the business mission. They have been inspired by your passion and have internalized it. Now, unleash the power of their enthusiasm as focused action. They want to participate and fulfill their purpose with you. Provide them with various opportunities to fully participate.

This means providing them freedom to act in specific circumstances and allowing them to have a voice. Having a voice doesn't mean just an opportunity to speak; it means the opportunity to be heard and a chance to see their ideas become reality. If you have rock stars on your team, and you'd better, they will have creative ideas to help serve your customers, to make the office run smoother, to make things more efficient, to provide better energy, to improve the customer experience. Give them the opportunity to share their ideas and respond to them. Really listen, be appreciative, and implement the ideas that make sense. Many of them will.

Here are some basic strategies to allow your team to be ongoing, active participants in fulfilling the business mission and generating great service.

# Empower Your Team with Autonomy

*"Control leads to compliance; autonomy leads to engagement." ~ Daniel H. Pink*

Once your employees are fired up around your mission, you need to empower them to do their jobs with focus. In this section, we will work on strategies that allow them to excel. Empowering your team begins with you. You must ensure that your team members have the tools and the freedom or autonomy to act, to do their best work.

Without autonomy, your team is stifled and inefficient. They will not have the freedom to find their own passion or utilize their creativity. Productivity will suffer; it is time consuming to ask for permission for every little action. And, you miss the insights, perspectives, and creativity of an impassioned team.

When I work with controlling leaders, I always picture the business as a giant helium balloon. The balloon represents the business that is trying to grow and soar. The micromanager is running from side to side trying to fill the balloon all alone, trying to tie off all of the loose ends. The balloon is not able to rise. It simply is not a task that one individual can achieve. The true leader will give the team the freedom necessary to let the business expand and soar.

Picture what it feels like as a customer to engage with a handcuffed team. You call into a call center with your fingers crossed hoping to land a person who will champion your issue. To your dismay you realize immediately that the person on the other end of the line has no power at all. They are reading from a script. Their ability to help you is limited to the words on a few pages. You ask to speak to a manager or someone in authority only to find that there is no one there or, what a shock, that one person with power is busy and won't be able to get back to you for days. That one person with the freedom to act is tied up taking care of hundreds of small issues that could be handled swiftly by many if it were allowed.

Zappos.com, an online shoe store extraordinaire, provides a great illustration of a business providing excellent service through its people. The team at Zappos.com has the freedom to be creative in order to exceed customer expectations. They can send cards, send a truck to pick up a shipment, deliver flowers, or include a special gift in with a shipment of shoes. Each employee has complete discretion up to a specific cost limit. The team would not be as nimble if they had to ask permission for each little extra. Instead, the leaders leave these activities to the complete creative discretion of the team. The result is an empowered team providing awesome customer service and having fun while they do it.

Give your employees the autonomy to conduct some of their work without your direct supervision. You can and should set boundaries around what they can do without you. But if you have to be involved in every decision, your circle of influence is no greater than you, there is no opportunity for discretionary effort. Your team's ability to work quickly and creatively will be hampered if they have to wait for a conversation with you before every action.

Create firm definitions if you are uncomfortable.

- Set a maximum price for purchases made without your approval.

- Give them space to handle an unhappy customer. Provide the opportunity for discretion within a set list of possible responses, for instance. By allowing your team to provide a quick response, you can avoid escalated hurt feelings from the customer.

- Provide freedom to coordinate minor repairs or place orders to the discretion of a few. Internet outages or phone system repairs should not require the participation of a leader. Office supplies, business cards and other small purchases should be made from a budget managed by members of the team.

Difficulty in trusting your team can be about either your shortcomings or theirs. In a later section, you will analyze your team members to determine their ability to meet your mission effectively. If they are not currently able, you will create a game plan to get them there, either with your current team or with some new players. Remember, you cannot do it all on your own. If you find there are issues with you, we'll work through that as well. Either way, you will be moving towards an increased circle of influence and more action towards your mission.

It probably goes without saying, that to empower your team takes courage and trust as a leader. First, make sure they have the cornerstones of success in place. If the basics are not there, your delegation process cannot yield excellence. We will spend some time on each of the basic cornerstones of success. As always, though, you are ultimately responsible for correcting any shortfalls you identify.

## Catapult Task: Providing Autonomy

**I have a tendency to control the actions of my team under these circumstances:**

**I use these tactics to control the actions of my team:**

**My employees are impacted in this way when I fail to provide autonomy:**

**Our customers are impacted in these ways when I stifle productivity:**

**Our customers have to jump through these hoops to get their issues resolved when the team does not have freedom to act:**

**I minimize our ability to achieve in these ways:**

**I commit to providing autonomy in these areas:**

**I will others to make these kinds of purchases or coordinate these fixes without my participation (be specific about people and amounts):**

**I want to provide my team the autonomy to act on behalf of customers in these circumstances:**

**I will use these strategies to make it happen:**

# Empower Your Team with Good Communication

*"Much unhappiness has come into the world because of bewilderment and things left unsaid." ~ Fyodor Dostoyevsky*

Even in a fueled team, a lack of communication can cause frustration and act like a sedative. "I can't move because I don't know what is going on!"

Great communication, on the contrary, provides a catalyst to activity that is focused on mission and great service. "I know enough about what is going on and about our general direction to act independently, with the assurance that my efforts will be well coordinated with the overall mission." Communication gives courage and empowers your team to work with precision.

Here are some basic strategies to keeping your team well informed and nimble.

# Maintain a Good Meeting Rhythm

I cannot tell you the number of businesses I have seen with no consistent communication path. I find frustrated leaders and chaotic teams that have no focus. There is no opportunity to hold employees accountable because there is no way to verify if the employees actually knew what was going on in the business. How can a team find focus without information?

When your business is small, you and one or two other people, you can thrive on a communication process that consists of ad hoc conversations that you have in the hallway as you pass. However, once you get any larger than that, you need to invest some time in formalized communication streams.

I still believe that employees want to do a good job. However, in many of the businesses I have worked with, somehow the perfect storm was created: the wrong team, failure to hold team accountable or communicate clear expectations, tons of frustration and chaos, all of which leads to a group norm of, "It wasn't my fault." Employees begin to put energy toward avoiding accountability. The lack of communication also supplies many avenues for hiding from accountability, "I didn't know," "I never heard about that," "I wasn't at the meeting," "she never told me." And the truth is, you can't prove it because there is no documentation of communication. Does it even require stating it again? All of this creates drama.

Employee communication done well has the potential to:

- Encourage discretionary effort

- Reduce absenteeism

- Improve retention

- Increase efficiency

- Create great customer service

Providing clear direction will allow your team to work with tenacity.

Your team wants to know where you are going, how you will get there, and what role they will each play in the journey.

Hold regular team meetings with opportunity to communicate expectations and time to debate a bit. Remember, you have final authority. But really receive, hear, and consider input from your team. This opportunity for give and take really enhances the feeling of your team being on a mission together; it empowers them to participate fully. The added bonus, you may get some valuable input!

Assign accountability for communication to your leader(s). Let information cascade via a specified path through your organization. Communication, like all other important tasks, must be assigned to specific people so the ball is not dropped. Face to face communication is best and should be used when possible. This allows for efficient clarification and provides the benefit of non-verbal communication.

Create a system for communication that works and include a process that documents receipt. For instance, create a deadline for reviewing notes with a sign off sheet or require that employees email back to confirm understanding. Utilize the system consistently. Here are some strategies that have worked with my clients.

- Regularly scheduled in-person meetings with a good agenda

- An email blast

- Alerts posted in a specific spot

- Updates posted on your intranet

- Memos in mailboxes

- A communication log kept in a centralized notebook

## Team Huddle

The huddle is just another name for a quick, informal meeting. I am sure that the name derived from the football huddle that happens between plays. In football the huddle gives the team the opportunity to come together quickly to gain focus, create a strategy, and evaluate how the last play went. The quarterback also passes on information received from the coach.

I recommend that at least once a day, your team or a subset of them, have a huddle where employees can engage in quick problem solving, pass on pertinent information or determine any special customer needs that require focus for the day. Discuss any special circumstances, anything new, business goals, marketing strategies, and list process improvement needs. Start the day on a positive note and with an opportunity for good communication.

## Weekly Team Meetings

Make sure to allow time for good, effective team meetings. They are pivotal in your efforts to focus an empowered team. You should have at least one team meeting every other week, though once per week is better. I am never a proponent of having a meeting just to have a meeting. If you have ineffective meetings, they are a complete waste of time. The solution is not to stop having meetings, though. On the contrary, commit to having the meetings and then run them well so they *are* effective. Make them a priority. Tell your team that they must be on time and do the same yourself, if you attend the meeting. Assure that meetings start and end on time and that idol chit chat is kept to a minimum.

Here are some key topics to incorporate into your meeting agendas to assure that you are using your time well:

- **Allow time for education of employees by employees**: Every business I've worked with has the constant need to train team members. Whether it's new processes or regulations, new initiatives, or just keeping up with certifications, there is always something new to learn.

  Have you ever heard that the best way to learn is to teach? If you want members of your team to really excel, give them the opportunity to teach other team members. It saves you the time, gives them the motivation to really learn what they will teach, provides an opportunity to work a new muscle and take on a new challenge, and is a great way for your other employees to learn. If your team meetings have morphed into the *"You Show,"* trust me, they will welcome the opportunity to hear from their peers. It's a win – win – win!

- **Create time for process improvements:** The weekly team meeting is the perfect time to create issues lists that will become process improvement initiatives. You will not conduct much problem solving during the meeting. Rather, focus on assigning responsibilities and communicating updates. This item should be included on every agenda. We will discuss some simple process improvement techniques in a later chapter.

- **Discuss business goals:** Your employees want to participate in your mission. The purpose of team meetings is to communicate direction and celebrate success. Take the time to share any new business goals or progress on current goals. Or, perhaps your team will help to set a few goals. Ideally, you will have some key measures that can be discussed to determine progress; a weekly score card. For example, do you monitor weekly sales totals or new customers? Give your team the opportunity to generate ideas that help meet or exceed these goals.

- **Brainstorm "Wow customer service" ideas:** Harness your team's creativity and enthusiasm towards wowing your customers. Give them the opportunity to share ideas. Including this agenda item during each meeting will communicate the importance of this top objective. As a team you can pick which initiatives to focus on first and then assign members to work on implementation.

- **Generate marketing ideas:** I love to encourage my clients to include all employees in marketing strategies. At a minimum, they could hand out business cards to educate their network about the products and/or services you provide. Word of mouth is the best form of advertising and you should be taking full advantage.

  Encourage them to get creative about other strategies to educate the public about your offerings. How can they use social media? You have great products or services to provide and there are many people who could benefit. They can't benefit if they don't know. Have your team help spread the word. Make it a part of everyone's job.

  Of course, there will be some circumstances where marketing by word of mouth is not appropriate. Perhaps your employees can help you come up with new ideas to establish relationships with other businesses that offer related products or services and would be great referral partners, or some on your team may want to find events to participate in. Brainstorm about where your target market spends time or money.

- **Assign tasks and give deadlines:** I am not a proponent of solving problems in weekly meetings unless it is a team issue; but you should assign responsibilities and give deadlines for problem solving during these meetings. The real work happens separate from team meetings with only key players. There is no need to monopolize the time of your entire team if only a few need to be involved.

- **Design an interactive meeting that involves communication in both directions:** This is a key goal of any meeting. Provide time for communication in both directions on the topics listed above and any others that are relevant. Meetings are for interaction and should be only part lecture.

## Catapult Task: Communication Strategies

**I have identified these issues with our current communication:**


**Our communication shortfalls result in these issues:**


**I will create these communication paths:**


**I will build accountability into our communication process in these ways:**


**I will make these changes to our team meetings:**


**I commit to these changes to improve communication:**

# Empower Your Team with Solution-Centered Communication

*"Focus 90% of your time on solutions and only 10% of your time on problems." ~ Anthony J. D'Angelo*

As you begin to encourage more and more communication, make sure your team meetings never morph into complaint sessions. I have seen far too many cultures support whining. And that activity definitely falls into the drama category!

Instead, create a focus around finding solutions. If there are issues to discuss, document the items, then assign ownership of fixing each item on the list. Or, adopt the policy that no one identifies an issue without also offering a solution. We will cover some simple process improvement strategies in more detail later. For now, just focus on the communication you are having with your team around issues. Begin to encourage the solution-centered thinking.

I often suggest a "Gripe and Grumble Form," to my clients. A sample is below. They work well because they emphasize the solution, not just the complaint. The easiest part of the improvement process is pointing out the flaws. The real meat is in coming up with solutions. Employees have a tendency to modify their complaints accordingly if they are required to provide solutions as well. They will make sure that it is worth the effort.

Here is the sample Gripe and Grumble Form. Put your logo at the top, you can fit two to a page.

# Turn a Gripe or a Grumble into a Request or a Solution

It's easy to complain, gripe, or grumble. But it takes energy without getting you anywhere and sucks energy from those around you.

If your gripe or grumble is worth spending any energy on, then it's worth a bit of time and energy to fix. If it's not worth your energy to fix it, then it's not worth your energy to gripe about.

If you have a gripe or grumble that is worthy, fill out the form, come up with a solution or request and give it to the office manager. Either way, get it off your chest!

**Gripe/Grumble:**

**Request/Solution:**

## Catapult Task: Solution-Centered Communication

**The team has these tendencies when it comes to discussing issues:**

**I will focus the team on solution-centered communication in these ways:**

# Empower Your Team with Clear Expectations

*"A civilization is built on what is required of men, not on that which is provided for them." ~ Antoine de Saint Exupéry*

Your team is fueled and ready to act. You don't want a fueled team acting spontaneously without direction. Continue to hone their focus with communication. You need them heading toward the specific targets you create. Expectations, clearly communicated, create the focus for that fuel.

As I've stated before, I like to work under the assumption that employees want to do a good job. As a leader it is your job to define what success looks like. Spelling out specific and clear expectations for your team will give them a target to aim for, a clear focus. It will build confidence and allow them to take action without specific ad hoc instruction.

Ultimately, it's making sure each employee is working in concert with the business goals and objectives. This can mean documenting everything from huge initiatives as a goal or expectation, to the smallest rule about cell phone use. Your employees feel more confident if they know where the boundaries are.

We will begin very simply with the basics of a job description, why you should have a complete policy manual, and what should be included in an attendance policy. Then we will discuss additional strategies for assuring you are communicating clear expectations aligned with your mission and vision. The goal is to know that your employees have a clear sense of how they can make an impact and what they are accountable for personally.

# Communicate Clear Expectations with a Job Description

A job description is a great way to create focus. We've talked about mission-centered job statements already and those are a great way for your employees to think about their jobs in order to get that motivation flowing. A traditional job description will help them get clear on the types of activities they will engage in to achieve those outcomes. In other words, it will provide a nice outline of how they will be spending their time on the job. At a minimum, you have a basic list of responsibilities. Of course, there is always an, "other duties as assigned" disclaimer. A job description does not give a reason to say no to work. But, generally speaking, what are your expectations of them; what will they be doing, how quickly must they work, what level of quality is required? Be sure to include specifics about how the role can impact the customer experience as well.

It is also helpful to know how each job fits into the big picture.

If you don't already have a full job description, don't worry. You'll be brushing the dust off of what you have or starting from scratch to create up to date descriptions for each position in a later chapter.

# Communicate Clear Expectations with a Company Policy Manual

There are expectations specific to each job and those that apply for the company as a whole. Both are important. A good policy manual allows you to set consistent standards across departments and locations and is a great tool to invite new employees into your business culture. You want the intentional, written standards to win, over the unwritten group norms that may be inconsistent with your goals.

## Areas to Include in a Policy Manual

Even if you have just one employee, you should have a basic policy manual for your office. It provides a simple mechanism for communicating the basic rules of engagement for your business and culture. Here are some areas that you may wish to cover:

- Cell phone use

- Internet access

- Attendance

- Smoking

- Dress codes

- Basic customer service standards

- How employees should treat each other

- Treatment of company property

- Drug & Alcohol use

- Employee communication

Have a professional assist you with your policy manual. It is an important document that includes locally or federally governed policies that change frequently. I have not included these in the list above.

Your policy manual should also spell out the specific consequences of failure to comply. Remember, your employees want to do a good job. You define what doing a good job looks like. Start with the basics first, then define what it means to do a good job for each position.

## Attendance Policy:

Many of my smaller clients do not have an attendance policy. I believe, however, that a good attendance policy is a must. Too often, attendance becomes an issue for employees and a source of resentments among team members, in other words, drama. Clearly spell out a rule for the number of times an employee can be absent, how often he or she can be tardy and, as always, communicate the consequences for failure to comply. Providing this level of detail will give your employees the opportunity to choose well. Your rock stars will also be happy with the prospect of a reduced need to pick up slack during absenteeism or tardiness.

A good policy provides for a reasonable number of absences and some tardiness. Life does happen. If you structure it well, you do not have to get into the game of determining whether the excuse was legitimate. All excuses have equal weight so there is no subjectivity.

# Communicate Clear Expectations
# with Customer Service Objectives

*"Do what you do so well that your customers will want to see it again and bring their friends." ~ Walt Disney*

A remarkable team, fully aligned with a mission and an outward focus on customers, does not have time to gossip, worry about who is doing what, or who is on their cell phone. They will be working like a well-oiled machine, fueled and fully engaged on their purpose. Do all you can to focus your team on customer service. Make a game of reaching hefty goals weekly or monthly; constantly remind them of the importance of their work. Each member of your team needs to know the value of their position and its role in providing great service. Each employee needs to know how he or she can help enhance the customer experience. Keep the focus on the ever-increasing goal of improving customer service.

You also must place emphasis on the concept of internal customer service. Some in your organization serve fellow employees in pursuit of great external service. The needs of an internal customer must, then, carry the same weight as those of an external customer. All must be empowered with knowledge of what it takes to be successful.

## Catapult Task: Communicating Clear Expectations

**We have fallen short in communicating clear expectations in these ways:**



**Our issues with clear expectations have robbed our team of focus in these ways:**



**We will do the following with job descriptions to make sure that they communicate expectations:**

**We commit to utilizing customer service expectations.**

**We fall short in these areas with our policy manual:**

**I commit to documenting and formalizing our unwritten office rules.**

**I see these areas where it would be helpful to have established guidelines:**

**We commit to making these changes to make sure that we have consistent, company-wide work standards.**

**These positions have direct customer service:**

**These roles have more internal customers than external:**

**We will communicate about and focus on internal customer service in these ways:**

**Our organization expects this level of service for its external customers:**

〜ᴔᇬ〜

# Communicate Clear Expectations
# with Great Delegation

*"Surround yourself with the best people you can find,*
*delegate authority, and don't intervene." ~ Ronald Reagan*

It sounds so simple; just tell people what to do. But, many leaders struggle in this area. It's hard to relinquish control. Many times, leaders I work with, feel discouraged because they don't get the results they want when they ask employees to perform a task. Too often, they give in and decide it is easier to do it themselves.

The problem is that this sets a precedent with the team. "I don't need to do a thorough job. My boss takes over and finishes anyway." Or, "My boss double checks it anyway. I don't really need to worry about getting it right." Or, worse yet, "Why bother starting it? She ends up taking it back and doing it anyway. I'll just wait for that to happen rather than waste my time."

If you have kids, you already know this phenomenon. If you ask your child to do something three times and then start yelling at them to get moving and this is your pattern, you have taught your child to move only when you start yelling. Or, you tell your child no and they start to whine, then cry, and then throw themselves on the floor.

If you give in and give them what they want at this point, they have learned that the quicker they throw themselves on the floor, the quicker they get what they want.

You've heard it before, "We teach people how to treat us." Even when you have the best of intentions, you can end up creating an ineffective culture. And, if this is how you are operating your business, your team members are frustrated and feel mistrusted, while you are angry and overwhelmed.

I always assume that people want to do a good job and like the feeling of a job well done. If you are not allowing your team to function at their highest potential, you are robbing them of the opportunity to feel fully successful. Employees who are not able to feel successful end up feeling frustrated and resentful, not the optimum emotions for a drama free workplace. Delegating work that stretches the capabilities of your team will catapult their success, fire them up, and will create an environment where excellence is the standard.

You need to create a culture where your team members feel accountable for their work and have opportunity to excel. You also want to foster a no-excuses or just-get-it-done mentality. And, like everything else we've been talking about, it begins with you. You need to do some reality checking to see what part you are playing in creating a culture where it is acceptable to give it less than your all.

The good news is delegating is a simple process. And, if it's a struggle for you to delegate, don't worry. Every leader I've ever worked with, and there are many, has been missing at least one of these key elements. It is usually possible to transform your delegation style with just a small tweak.

The goal is to delegate well and then let go. Communicate exactly what needs to be done, by when to create that clear expectation. We will go over the simple steps of delegation. If you are already starting to feel a panic attack coming on or are thinking that the entire business will fall down in shambles if you let go of your activities, don't worry. We'll create a step-by-step process that allows you to take only small steps, if necessary, to get where you ultimately need to be. You can start practicing these steps with some teeny, tiny activities. If you follow each step correctly, you will experience success. Take note of that success, and then delegate some bigger, more important tasks. As you feel success with those, delegate bigger tasks, and then projects. Before you know it you will be confidently delegating tasks left and right.

Here are the important steps in order:

## What

Take time to get clear about what you are delegating so you can succinctly communicate it to your team.

- Specifically what is it that you will delegate?

- Is it an entire project or is it a task'?

- Where does this fit in the scope of the business?

- What outcome will it create?

- What difference do you need to see?

- What standard of quality needs to be met?

# Who

Select one employee who will be 100% accountable for making sure that this task or project gets completed. They may not be the only one working on it. As a matter of fact, they may not actually do any of the work. But, by delegating to this person, he or she is fully accountable for ensuring that it is done on time and correctly. And ultimately, this is what you want. If multiple people are accountable, there is too much opportunity for finger pointing or passing the buck, "I thought she was going to do it."

Sending a blanket delegation to your team is like a bride throwing a bouquet. You don't want to turn your back, close your eyes and toss. You are leaving it to chance that someone will catch it and go. Sometimes this works, but more often it just falls to the floor. Instead, you want to treat delegation like the Olympic Torch runner. You want to pass the task to one person who will be a good steward of the responsibility. And once passed, you must let go. The last torch runner does not run alongside or continue to hold on. They pass it and stop. Go on to the next thing.

I always use the term, "moving it off your plate." And that is the goal. We want to completely take the task or project off your plate and out of your brain space. You must completely let go. If you are still worrying, brainstorming, considering, checking in or anything else with regard to a task or project you have delegated, then you have not let it go. Ultimately, you are leaving yourself accountable. It's still on your plate and your team knows it. You cannot create a new culture without changing yourself. Begin now.

If you are thinking that there is no one on your team qualified to take on this project or task then it is time to do some reality checking. Really? You are truly the only one capable? Have you made poor hiring choices or have you failed to invest in appropriate training? Because, once again, it all comes back to you. The answer can no longer be, "They can't do it." That is not a sustainable way to run a business or lead a department.

Now is the time to fix it either by:

- Changing your mindset and releasing control immediately or over time

- Training existing employees based on the Catapult Task you will complete shortly

- Starting from scratch

Your success depends on your ability to trust your employees. The Lone Ranger cannot accomplish as much as a general with a platoon of soldiers.

## How (Optional)

This portion is optional. If you are delegating to a seasoned team member, they may already know how to do the job. It might come off as condescending for you to provide the step-by-step instructions. However, if you are delegating to someone new to the work it may be necessary to provide some detail. Where will they get the information? What phone numbers will they need to call?

Remember, the ultimate goal of great delegation is getting the job done efficiently and done right. Make sure that they have all the information they need.

Unfortunately, I have seen some leaders who get a kick out of watching their team struggle with a project. Sometimes it's an ego thing. If this is you, it is not effective! You are letting your ego win and the business lose.

## By When

Communicate a specific deadline. Giving a task and saying, "Get this done when you can," does NOT communicate a sense of urgency. If you are delegating with this kind of language, no wonder you are feeling frustrated. "When you get a chance," usually does not happen because there is no real call to action. You may intend to be nice or to acknowledge that your employee is busy. Or maybe you really want them to prioritize the work themselves. Ultimately, though, what they are hearing is, "this is not a big deal." And you end up feeling like you can't delegate anything because your stuff never gets done.

If you are delegating a larger project, create some intermediate deadlines along with the final deadline.

## Create a Communication Schedule

This is the step most often missed in the delegation process. And it is a very important, especially as you work to build your delegation muscle. When you delegate the task and deadline, create a communication loop by requesting that the delegate provide updates at specific intervals.

You want to offload this part of the process. If you don't, you have not fully delegated because you end up creating this scenario: On Monday, you ask someone to do a project. You tell them the deadline is one week from this Thursday. By Friday, you will begin thinking to yourself, "I wonder how they are doing on that project? Man, I really hope that they get it done on time. If they don't, it will really mess up...fill in the blank." You begin to think and worry about it more and more. Finally, you go to your employee to ask them, "How is that project coming?"

The problem is two-fold. One, the project is still taking up your brain-space. You have not fully offloaded it. You still actually own it. Your energy is still being used. Two, when you constantly go to your employees to ask or remind, you set a precedent that they don't need to worry about a project you delegate because you will remind them and may even offer assistance. In this scenario, they are not motivated towards excellence.

As an alternative, tell your delegate, "The project is due a week from this Thursday. By Friday, I want you to send me an email detailing the progress you have made. On Tuesday, we will sit down for 15 minutes to cover where you are and any support you need from me or other team members."

Now, you can sit back and relax knowing that the employee is fully accountable for the project and for providing you with updates. You do not need to ask. They have fully taken on the responsibility.

When you first start to delegate this way, it may feel very uncomfortable to let go and wait for updates. If this is the case, don't give up. Just take a smaller step. Make the intervals between updates shorter. If you need an update daily, set that as the standard. Slowly you will build confidence in yourself and in your team. The more success you experience with delegating, the easier it will become. Soon you will be delegating and requesting very few updates. You will have set the stage for an environment where your team is fully accountable and you are comfortable and confident in their abilities and follow-through.

## Offer Your Support Up-Front

As part of your No Excuses campaign, you must offer support up-front and then let it go.

Make it very clear that an excuse like, "I couldn't get it done. I didn't have time," will not fly. The employee accountable for the project must inform someone if he or she is falling behind and must ask for assistance. Assistance can come from you, if it is initiated by the delegate. If you continue to offer your support you are, once again, designing an environment that assumes you will step in or come to the rescue. And saying nothing about the deadline might create an assumption that it's okay to miss it. It is not a drop-dead deadline. You don't want to leave an employee with the out of, "Oh, I didn't know I was supposed to tell you ahead of time that I wouldn't get it done."

# What to Delegate

One of the privileges of leadership is being able to delegate the tasks you do not want to do, or that you are not good at. But don't just take advantage of it because you can, take advantage because it's a smart business decision. We all have gifts we are born with. I like to think of them as God-given talents. We should be spending at least 80% of our time on the areas of our gifting. The rest, if possible, should be delegated to others. You have people in your business who have gifts that are complimentary to yours. Doesn't it make sense to allow them to do things they are best at, too?

Think about tasks that you do on a routine basis now that are a struggle for you. They zap your energy or you might employ creative procrastination techniques to avoid doing them. These are key tasks to focus on as you create your delegation list.

## Catapult Task: Commitment to Delegate

**These tasks zap my energy and take me away from what I do best:**

**I am not very good at these tasks; others do them much better than me:**

**I have these resources available to delegate to (include team members, trusted advisors, and service providers):**

**I commit to delegating these tasks to these specific people:**


**I will get out of my comfort zone at least 3 times in the next week to delegate more:**


**I commit to using all the key steps to the delegation process:**


**I have had these successes:**

# Energize Your Team for Fire

*"Energy and persistence alter all things." ~ Benjamin Franklin*

Your team is fueled and focused. Energy is the fire. It is time to re-move the barriers to unbridled action and generate the energy that will be used to create great customer care. Make sure they have every opportunity to turn their focused actions into success. Allow them to harness their abilities, benefit from the momentum their passion generates, and to use everything they've got as an accelerator for the business.

There are two main ingredients to providing great service. The first ingredient is the customer experience your team provides through their behaviors and enthusiasm. The second ingredient is the logistics of service. Your team must have both to stay energized. They are on fire and enthusiastic about serving your customers. It is frustrating for a team to have a leader serve up a goal that they are unable to achieve because of variables outside their control.

Assure that nothing stands in their way or causes them to lose motivation. Processes must function well and be well aligned with the objectives of the business. Each employee must have the knowledge, skills, and abilities to be successful, and the time and resources to create the right outcomes.

In this section you'll work through identifying and removing any barriers that exist to your team's full achievement and then implement strategies to generate energy.

## Remove Barriers to Achievement to Energize Your Team

*"Obstacles are those frightful things you see when you take your eyes of your goal." ~ Henry Ford*

I've stated it before but it bears repeating. For some reason, humans assign work difficulties to people, whether fault rests there or not. Thus, to defeat the drama and create a fired up team, we must remove the barriers that limit the team's ability to achieve. In this section, we will cover the logistics of service that impact your team's ability to achieve. Do the individual team members have what they need to be successful? Are the systems of service in place and sound?

Your team may have the best intentions, but if they face constant challenges or barriers that stand in the way of success, you will have drama.

As a leader, to defeat the drama, you must champion removing challenges so your team can function well and achieve.

There is enough natural potential for drama as humans interact. Different personalities and misunderstandings cause enough trouble. Do not add another layer of complexity by requiring your team to function in and around barriers to efficient work.

The first potential barrier to success we'll look at is whether or not your individual team members have what it takes to be successful. Do they have the required knowledge, skills, and abilities? What about the personality it takes to provide the customer service you desire? If not, can they get there? What specific steps must they follow to get there? Is it training, reading, job shadowing? Do they need an attitude adjustment? In this section, you will figure that out so you can remove any individual barriers to success.

The cornerstones of success we will cover are:

1.  Knowledge, Skills, Abilities & Personality

2.  Resources

3.  Processes

4.  Time

# Assess Knowledge, Skills, Abilities, and Personality (KSAP's)

*"The only real security that a man will have in this world is a reserve of knowledge, experience, and ability." ~ Henry Ford*

In a prior section we covered the importance of communicating expectations with a job description. In this section you will use the contents to evaluate each team member. If you have made it this far into the book and still do not have job descriptions now is the time to hunker down and do it. You must have at least a basic understanding of what it takes to be a rock star in each position. Formalizing this step provides the building blocks for everything else that happens with your team.

A job description, whether formal or basic will:

- Drive the hiring process. What will you look for during the interview process to identify that future superstar who will fit well in your organization?

- Determine what training is required at time of hire.

- Provide a standard for measuring performance.

- Help you create a performance-based compensation plan and a career path.

- Give you a basis for evaluating each employee's performance abilities and help you identify where to utilize additional training resources.

- Help you make a better decision about whether a new employee should continue employment beyond their introductory period.

- Allow you to evaluate your employees based on set standards.

- Give you the confidence to become an influential delegator.

For your current team, you want to assure that each has the building blocks they need to provide great service. They cannot function on all cylinders if they are missing any of the key ingredients for success. You want every team member to be fully energized. First, identify all that is required to be successful, including personality. Then, we will walk through evaluating each team member and creating a plan of action where there are deficiencies. In a later chapter, I will walk you through strategies for communicating the plan.

## Catapult Task: KSAP Exercise 1 – Document the Requirements of each Job

A human resource manager, office manager, or other designated person, can help you with this section.

Pull together what you have for job descriptions. Then pick a job, any job, and take a fresh look. Does it include all major tasks? Does it include the behaviors and personality traits required to provide great service? If there is anything missing, add it.

If you do not have a job description, a great place to start is on the Internet. Google search or go to job sites like careerbuilder.com or monster.com for examples. Use what you find as samples for a starting point and tweak from there to fit your organization's specific needs. Or, you may want to bring in a trusted advisor. A consultant will have the experience to help you create top notch, professional descriptions that capture the essence of the job and meet any federal or state requirements.

Also, go back to your Ultimate Customer Experience Catapult Task. You identified key personality traits and behavior requirements there. Make sure to include those now.

Once you have all the tasks written down, take a fresh look at the training required.

- Are there certifications or education mandated by either state or federal regulations?

- Are there education, training, and certifications classes that must be completed prior to hiring into the position?

- Is there training that must be satisfactorily completed in-house for your employee to meet the minimum qualifications?

- What temperaments or behaviors does a team member have to have to be a rock star in the position?

    o Do they need to be detail-oriented or customer service focused?

    o Do they need to be flexible or follow strict guidelines?

○ Do they need to be able to multitask and stay calm in a fast-paced environment or do you need a self-starter who will find things to do during inevitable downtime.

○ What works best for your environment and culture?

○ Who do they need to be to work well with you and other leaders?

○ What behaviors must they exhibit to create your defined customer experience?

○ What personality traits are required to fulfill your customer service focus?

I have helped staff many businesses and it is important to get real about your own personality and quirks as a leader. If you are a fly-by-the-seat-of-your-pants, let-it-flow, tell-you-last-minute, change-your-mind-all-the-time, kind of leader, you are going to have conflict with a rigid employee.

You may need that person, though!

However, you will bump heads, so you must complete a self-evaluation to get real. If you are hiring your opposite, you must anticipate and navigate any resulting conflict. You must let them know about your personality during the interview process, so they can make an informed decision. A candidate with an accurate description of the environment they are entering has a much better chance of being successful and sticking it out.

Or, maybe you don't want that kind of friction. You may only want fly-by-the-seat-of-their-pants employees. Just get real about it here.

You will need to complete this process for each job in your business or department. Even if you don't end up with a formal, final draft of a beautiful job description, you at least need the list of minimum knowledge, skills, abilities, and personality traits required for success in each job. Remember to use language that attaches to your mission!

At some point, do plan to have good solid job descriptions that meet all requirements for federal regulations such as the Americans with Disabilities Act (ADA), for example.

## Catapult Task: KSAP Analysis Exercise 2 – Evaluate The People

Once you have completed the KSAP analysis for each job, evaluate the person in each position. Please complete each of these steps. These are important building blocks to the next steps!

Again, you may want to have a human resource employee or other trusted advisor help you. Or, if you have an office manager, supervisor, or other team member who helps you with human resource functions you might have them assist. *A word of caution though,* they must be mature enough to keep this process completely confidential. Furthermore, they must feel confident in their own abilities or be open to learning if they have room to grow in their own position. You need to be real with them as well. Do some reality checking here! I have been in many businesses where an office manager is a source of many of the problems with the culture. The key to doing the exercise for maximum results is to get real and protect no one.

This is not about being vindictive or mean. It is about doing a reality check and making your customers the number one priority. You have big things to accomplish and you need the right team functioning at their highest levels to create the biggest benefit for those who need your services or products.

Did I hit a nerve? Were you cringing as you read that paragraph or did you feel defensive? If so, you may not want to bring your office manager or supervisor in for this process. Even if you do not allow them to participate in their own evaluation, they will know you are doing it. If they are open to critique and willing to grow into the position as it needs to exist in your new world, let them in. If they are defensive and unwilling to bend or change, you may want to keep this evaluation on the down-low. Call in a trusted advisor from the outside instead. Sometimes it is easier to get real when you have an unbiased outside party.

Do not worry; you are not going to make any final decisions yet. You are just starting to empower yourself by beginning to evaluate your options with your team. The good news is, it will be a winning situation for you regardless. You may have to navigate some tough decisions or actions to get there. On the other side, however, is a full focus on passion and mission. It's worth it!!

Okay, enough pushing from me; create a form similar to the one below or use an Excel spreadsheet to quickly document your initial thoughts about your team.

Write down the name and job title of each member of your team on your form.

| Employee Name | Job Title | KSAP's | +, - , = | Action |
|---|---|---|---|---|
|  |  |  |  |  |
|  |  |  |  |  |
|  |  |  |  |  |

Honestly and as objectively as possible, go through your list of employees one by one and compare their current level of knowledge, skills, abilities, and personality to what is required of the position.

As you conduct this analysis, record where they excel and where they have shortfalls.

Where there are shortfalls, determine what is required for them to function at the level you need them to function. Is it training from an external source? Is it additional time shadowing a co-worker, or do they maybe need an attitude adjustment? Be as specific as possible. What investment is required by you, your organization, and by them? Make a note in the Action column.

Determine whether it is realistic for them to make the required changes. Are they willing? You may not know the answer to this yet. If you have not yet required them to function at an excellent level, if you've been allowing them to skate, allowing them to vent or cause drama, you do not necessarily know what they are fully capable of if the rules change or if a job is on the line. But, take a first best guess about whether or not it is doable.

Is their personality misaligned with the requirements of the position? Misaligned behaviors, if a result of attitude issues, are difficult or impossible, to change. Much of our personality is wired in us or has been formed over years.

If the answer is no, you do not feel that they can rise to the challenge of working to your new standards, the next question is, can they meet the exceptional standards of any other position in your business? Maybe they are a real whiz at part of their job. There may be a way to restructure or move them to allow them to reach their full potential with you. Important to note, however, you can not create a position to meet the needs of an individual employee. Positions are created to meet the needs of the organization. I am not suggesting that you make up a position to fit the needs of a mis-aligned employee.

Perhaps, you have an employee or two who are doing very well in every aspect of their job. There may be an opportunity to provide them with some job enrichment or career advancement.

## Document with a Performance Improvement Plan:

As you go through your evaluative process you will almost certainly identify individual issues that must be addressed. You will need to document the information and then have a private conversation with each employee. A great place to document these issues and follow up actions is on a Performance Improvement Plan document. A Performance Improvement Plan (PIP) is a written agreement between an employee and his/her manager that identifies opportunities for growth and the expectations for improvement over a specified period. I like to think of a PIP as a positive correction. You are documenting changes and learning what an employee must do to meet the standards of his or her job. You are also making a promise to them to help them improve. So, you are making a commitment to invest in their growth and helping them remove any known barriers to success.

In the PIP, you or the supervisor will spell out specifically what behaviors or skills need to be modified, any steps required to get there, and deadlines. The PIP will also identify specific training activities that an employee must complete. The employee and supervisor will schedule and document routine meetings to assess progress. The number of meetings and intervals will be determined by the extent of change required and the duration of the training.

It is also important to give the employee full accountability for keeping the scheduled meetings, requesting additional help, etc. The employee is responsible for reporting any circumstances that impedes his/her ability to successfully complete the guidelines of the PIP. You must communicate all of this succinctly.

The PIP can be done in conjunction with your discipline process if appropriate but can also stand alone. Or it can be used as a way of documenting necessary change identified during an annual performance management communication meeting.

If used in conjunction with discipline, the PIP does not affect the progression of the disciplinary process. It is not considered to be a step in that process. However, failure to adhere to the agreement spelled out in the PIP can result in disciplinary action.

You can find a sample Performance Improvement Plan in the Appendix.

## Other Barriers to Success

Now you will be looking more specifically at how your business infrastructures impact your team's ability to work independently and to be successful. And how they might impact the dynamics between people to create drama.

## Resources

Lacking resources is a potential barrier to success that can cause drama. Do you have: equipment that works well, effective forms, phone systems, office supplies, data management tools, space? You cannot gain full efficiency without the right resources. Take some time to evaluate your current resources. Make a list of any shortfalls. You can ask your team for input here. Do a cost-benefit analysis to determine the items in which you will invest.

Limited resources can leave your team fighting for those resources to do their jobs well. They will pit one against the other, creating drama.

## Time

Does your team have the time to do their jobs well or are they always rushing to get everything done? There is a fine line between hitting your maximum productivity and overwhelming your team completely. Are you realistic about what can be accomplished? Can you provide consistent deadlines or are emergencies constantly sidelining your top tasks? Moving targets and unrealistic deadlines encourage drama as employees fight to meet them, sometimes to the detriment of the team or customers.

Do you have margin in your schedule to allow for ad hoc issues, customer complaints, team communication, team building, meetings, planning, process improvement, Q & A time with leaders and all of the other activities that are part of a business?

I once worked with a client who scheduled every employee from start of day to end and beyond. There was no time for spontaneity of any sort. A request for additional time from a customer became a huge undertaking for the Executive Assistant who had to move other appointments around to accommodate. She was under constant pressure to squeeze time from a full schedule. Employee paths rarely crossed so there was no time for communication. If problem resolution of any kind required more than one team member the issue could not be resolved for weeks. If a customer called with an issue there was no extra time to get back with them for days. Return calls were generally made in the car on the way to or from work where there was no access to the data required to address customer concerns. Employees were 100% engaged in doing work so had no time to contemplate work. No time to evaluate processes, create sound strategies. The team was not cohesive and couldn't be. Relationships and building trust takes time. Drama was high and there was no solution given the current schedule.

Generating great service requires time. It is a valuable resource that must be used well.

# Processes

*"Stand up to your obstacles and do something about them. You will find that they haven't the strength you think they have." ~Norman Vincent Peale*

Is there a logical flow to your work or are you under constant chaos? Do you work around the same issues or errors day after day? Is there a good communication system? Are systems in place to support the customer experience you want to produce? Where do you need to focus to gain additional efficiency? Create a list. Next we will discuss the additional steps in conducting a simple but effective process improvement system. The truth is that process issues impact not only productivity but also employee relationships. I have seen it time and time again with my clients, failing processes translate into workplace drama. People have a tendency to assign fault to people when things go awry before considering that the issue is a result of flawed processes.

Here is a simple illustration that will help you identify where this might be happening in your organization. I worked with a team where everyone held disdain for an Administrative Assistant. They all felt that she was slow to respond when they needed information from her. The belief was that she was hoarding information to make their jobs more difficult and to build her own importance. So, in their minds it was all very purposeful.

Upon further digging, however, I found that this Administrative Assistant actually had a desire to help but had *the worst* process for organizing and retrieving information that I've ever seen!

As I evaluated the situation she shared that her process for organizing important information was to write it in an old calendar. "In the alphabetized section in the back of an old calendar?," I asked. No, that was not the case. I finally had her bring me her system to I could understand. What I saw was astonishing! When she said she kept her information in an old calendar she literally meant on the pages of an old calendar. She was basically utilizing the pages like scratch paper to randomly document her pertinent information across the dated boxes on the pages. There was no particular order. Names and phone numbers dotted the pages in upward and downward swoops. Some were written horizontally while others fell vertically.

Of course her retrieval process was laborious as a result. When team members asked her for information a swift response was impossible. The team assigned the delay to malicious intent rather than a poor process. Who, in this digital age, would assume that anyone would be using a disorganized hand written system?

Communication with the team about her desire to do well and some assistance with a more efficient process and that drama was defeated!

In other instances I have seen failing processes impact the dynamics between departments. This creates a similar scenario across an entire organization. For instance, a call center that set up appointments for several clinics lacked the information required to answer simple questions or schedule appointments effectively. The clinic staff, who often had to field questions from the call center as a result, felt that the team was just trying to forward their work on. A couple of meetings, barriers to service identified, the situation was resolved and the two teams were working well and serving customers harmoniously.

So, address your process issues. You'll get the double bonus of higher productivity and less drama.

Improving processes that you have identified as problematic does not have to be difficult. In a nutshell, analyze your processes to make them work better. There are very complex systems for evaluating processes, like Six Sigma, but you do not need to get that technical. You can keep it very simple and still reap the rewards.

Your goal is to create a team of "Solution Seekers," my term for employees who will think outside the box to solve problems. If you or your leadership teams are the only ones fixing issues, you are missing out! You have lost the opportunity for swift action as you become a stop gate for change. You've lost the opportunity to benefit from different perspectives throughout the work group as well as the creativity that flows from different individuals with varying strengths, backgrounds, education, and experience. The creative potential taps out at what leaders have to offer. On the contrary, you want to reap the benefit of the full compliment of perspectives, ideas, experiences, and creative abilities. In Mastermind Groups this is called tapping the third brain, the elevated creativity that is produced by a group of individuals all sharing their unique insights.

At a minimum, begin by working together to create a list of issues, common errors, hiccups, or barriers that impede your ability to reach goals and provide great service. Once you have your list, allow your team to prioritize which issues they want to tackle first. I always recommend starting with a few that are easy to improve but will have a big positive impact. I call it the "big bang for the buck" test. This gives your team some quick success and will motivate them to keep going. Carve out time weekly or monthly for team participation. These activities are win – win – win! Your team will have the opportunity to brainstorm improvements for your business. During that brainstorm, they will get to know each other better. If you have a larger business with at least several different departments, it will give your employees the chance to learn more about what others do day-to-day. From that knowledge, will grow learning and understanding. They will also begin to see the larger picture of how other departments or employees affect their own jobs.

This knowledge, learning, and understanding lead to appreciation. They will begin to know each other, their coworkers' strengths, and their contributions. Your team will start to connect. They will get excited about the work they are doing. They will be united towards a common goal.

And, we haven't even gotten to the core outcome for which process improvement was designed, which is improving your business! You will experience that as well! Work flow, customer follow-up, data management, billing, safety initiatives, any process you take on as a team, will get better. Processes designed from a variety of perspectives are better! Each person in your business has a unique view of your systems. When you bring those views together and consider them before making a change, the result is beyond what one person can create. Your team will also be more committed to consistently using the new processes because they played a part in creating the change. They have ownership in the design.

Additionally, you will have more reasons to celebrate as you become more and more efficient.

Have someone on your team who is a good organizer maintain a running list of the processes you will take on. That way you won't lose longer projects or ones that must be put on hold at first. It will also give you a quick visual of your successes. I usually highlight projects as they are completed so that the team can easily see that they are making progress. In those tougher times when you feel like nothing is getting done, you can look back and say, "Wow, we've actually accomplished a lot!"

Here's an example of a table I use when I work with a team. You can easily create it in Word. Make sure this gets delegated to someone who will stay on top of it. Over time, the table will get quite large.

| Start Date | Issue | Actions | Driver(s) | Doer(s) | Updates/ Notes |
|---|---|---|---|---|---|
| 11/01 | No consistent protocol for new equipment | ~Create procedure documentation for new equipment ~Train employees ~Create maintenance schedule | Procurement Manager | Technical supervisor, maintenance supervisor, technician | Meeting scheduled for 12/05//2011 |
| 09/05/ | New customer follow up inefficient | ~evaluate CRM software ~implement ~create procedure manual ~train CSR's | Customer Service Supervisor | CSR Team, IT rep. | **DONE!** |

# Catapult Task: Analyze Team Resources

Let's get clear on whether your team has the tools to be successful. Consider the infrastructures of your business. Look at them from the perspective of your team. Do poor processes or limited resources minimize your ability to delegate to your team? Or do they limit the ability to be successful?

We are unrealistic about time in these areas:

Employees have difficulty meeting deadlines here:

We lack good margin in our schedule here:

Time issues cause drama in these ways:

Time issues negatively impact customer service in these areas:

We commit to making these changes around the resource of time:

We suffer from these resource scarcities:

Resource scarcity creates drama in these ways:

Customer Service is impacted in these ways as a result of resource scarcity:

**What do you commit to do to enact change in this area?**


**We experience these constant barriers, issues, hiccups, challenges:**


**What process improvement initiatives will you engage in?**


**What processes limit your team's ability to succeed?**


**What is the impact of your inefficient processes on your team or on your ability to delegate?**


**What do you commit to do to enact change in this area? What process improvement initiatives will you engage in?**


**A Channel is a method of communication. Examples are: walking in, phone, email, website, Facebook, text.**


**List the all of the channels that your customers use to access your product(s) or service(s) now then rate them.**

**Where do you need improvement?**

A Touchpoint is a point of interaction based on a specific human need in a specific time and place. What interactions do your customers have with you? Examples: purchase, request service, follow up with questions, get issues resolved, return faulty products.

List all of your Touchpoints and rate them.

**Where do you need improvement?**

Take a methodical look at each component of your customer service.

Look at this list and determine where you need to include any of these into new customer service strategies for your business:

- **Good Follow through**

- **Keeping your word; having good integrity**

- **Timely service and good communication**

- **Friendly greetings**

- An element of empathy when a customer is working through a challenge

- Accuracy in service or product quotes

- Phones answered quickly with a friendly greeting by people empowered to own the issue and follow up to help your customer traverse the inner workings of your organization

- A quick response to those speaking on behalf of a customer so that they can provide timely, accurate information.

Every employee must become a champion for your customers.

What team behaviors and personality traits will create this experience?

What activities must the team engage in to create this experience?

Where must you insert empathy to create a swift connection with your customers?

What other barriers exist to creating a great customer experience?

**Where does drama impact your ability to take great care of your customers?**

**Define anything else that needs to change to create a great customer experience:**

**What do you commit to do to enact change in this area? What process improvement initiatives will you engage in?**

# Hurdle the Barriers to Great Delegation to Energize Your Team

*"Few things help an individual more than to place responsibility upon him and to let him know that you trust him." ~ Booker Washington*

Poor delegation leads to team drama. If you are following the six steps to great delegation as described earlier but still find that delegating is not creating the results you want, it may be a result of one of these common barriers. Identify the issue so that you can fix it and defeat the drama and achieve. Because saying, "I'll just do it myself," is not the right answer! You only have so much capacity, period. If you are trying to do it all, your circle of influence is smaller than it could be, and you are probably overwhelmed and possibly resentful. It is time to do some reality checking again.

Below are some of the more predominant barriers to delegation I have encountered through my work with clients, with actions you can take to overcome them:

**Your Control Issues:** You have a fear of letting go. You feel like you must provide your input or everything will go awry. You have to know what's going on.

> **What it looks like:** You constantly ask employees what they are doing. You want to know details that really don't matter. You are unable to give them the autonomy to complete even the smallest task or make even the smallest decision without your input.
>
> Even when you delegate a task, you end up taking it back or jumping in to rescue. Fear grips you if you don't. Your employees may not even start projects you delegate because, why bother?
>
> Or you hire a professional and then proceed to tell them exactly how to do their job. Require them to do what you've done in the past. You end up with no change because you are limiting them to your knowledge base rather than tapping into theirs. Then you feel frustrated because you are paying for someone who is not adding value.
>
> **What it feels like:** You feel overwhelmed and your employees feel mistrusted, disengaged, and frustrated.

**What you can do:** Start slowly. Pick some very small tasks in the office and follow the delegation steps diligently. Do not step in, no matter what. Bite your tongue; sit on your hands. Do whatever it takes. And when an individual employee or group of employees completes the task, take note. Start creating a mental list of successes in your head or even on paper. As the list of successes grows, so will your confidence. You can let go! Things will get accomplished without you. You will start to feel some freedom from your fear and will enjoy spending more time in your passion. Begin to delegate bigger and bigger tasks. Then move to larger projects. Each success is a step in the right direction. As always, celebrate your progress!

**Perfectionism:** You envision one specific way that things should be done and one specific outcome, regardless of the task or project. There is no wiggle room, one way or no way. You cannot let go because they might not do it exactly as you would. While excellence should be the standard, sometimes there are multiple ways to reach it. Perfection is not realistic and is often the culprit of control issues. I always think of the mom who complains that she has to do all of the laundry because no one will fold the towels the way she wants. She stays stuck folding towels while her kids miss out on the opportunity to feel responsible and learn a life skill.

**What it looks like:** Nothing is ever good enough. You feel like your team members are inept because they don't meet your standards, but you can't ever get there either. Something is always wrong. You delegate a task and immediately look for additional nuances that you did not communicate. Immediately fill the void created by the delegation with worry and focus on variables around the project and the journey it should take to complete. What other pieces might go unfinished if you don't think of them and act? What other challenges must be anticipated and accounted for. You are always coming up with additional *what if* scenarios. Always jumping in to take over. You are overwhelmed and burning out.

**What it feels like:** Fear and disappointment is the result. Fear that things will not be good enough and disappointment in everyone around you as no one can meet your standards. There is always something not quite right. Always some variable you thought of that your team didn't. Blame. Your team feels paralyzed and frustrated. They can't do anything well enough, why bother? You feel overwhelmed because more falls on your shoulders. And you feel frustrated because nothing is ever right.

**What you can do:** Perfectionism can be a tough one to let go. There are often many layers of fear that create the phenomenon. Fear of making a mistake, fear of letting people down or disappointing them, fear of everything falling apart. Perfectionists often, *"what if"* their lives away. To work around this one, you just HAVE to start practicing letting go. Perfect standards are not realistic. You'll white knuckle it initially. But let your team complete a project without you. Or call something finished yourself before it is perfect. Sit back and wait for what will come. Rarely will the outcome be as bad as what you envisioned. Often, there will be no negative fallout at all! Sometimes, unbelievably, your team will come up with something BETTER than what you had envisioned!

As you experience mini successes, store them for ready access in your brain database or keep a list. These successes will build, and as they do, you'll feel more confident in just letting go. Slowly allow bigger and bigger tasks to be completed. Allow your team to take on bigger projects. Allow them the freedom to do it their way. Continue to grow that list of successes. Eventually, you will be getting a lot more done and feeling a lot less stress! Trust me on this! I've helped many leaders with this one and it IS better.

**You have the right team but they have not been properly trained:** You've done the reality checking. It is not that you are afraid to delegate. Your employees really do NOT have the skills to complete the work you need done. They are willing and want to help, work well together, have good positive attitudes, and the ability to learn. You just have not allotted the time required for you or another team member to train them.

> **What it looks like:** You are doing all the work or some things are not getting done because no one has the skills to do it. It looks like all the best intentions without any of the desired results.

> **What it feels like:** You are not as productive as you could be and neither is your team. It feels like constant barriers to getting things done. Your team is frustrated because they believe in your mission and want to help. They just aren't able to help as much as they could with the proper training.

> **What you can do:** Get them trained. Take a step-by-step approach. Work through the list you created in the earlier section when you evaluated your employees based on the

required Knowledge, Skills, and Abilities. Prioritize the list by the training that is most necessary and figure out a way to get it done. Do it yourself, assign the task to a team member, or send them out to get the knowledge that they need. If you have great team members, you want to invest in their success. Great employees eventually burn out if they don't feel successful. And they cannot feel successful if they do not have the skills to do their jobs well.

**You don't have the right team:** You've done the reality checking and it's not your fears or control issues that stops you from delegating. You have done a thorough job with the KSAP checklist in the previous section and have found that you just do not have the right team in place. You cannot delegate because they cannot do the work. Maybe you have provided the right training and they just don't get it. Or maybe they are missing that heart to serve and do not have the ability to care about your mission the way you need them to. They are unable to see what needs to be done or to take the initiative. Or maybe they are defensive and just don't want to take on anything new.

**What it looks like:** Chaos. You tell your team to do something. They don't respond. Or, maybe, you are to the point where you won't even try to ask for anything to avoid the attitudes. You are a lone ranger in a sea of employees. There is little coordination between you and them. They just do their own thing and you try to avoid contact. Or you ask for things and are ignored or experience conflict.

**What it feels like:** It feels like you have no power in your business. You are frustrated and resentful. Your employees realize either they are wrong and worry, or they don't care and act defensive. If they can maintain control, their jobs are safe.

**What you can do:** Take back your power! You might want to skip ahead in the book to the next section. The steps there will help you begin weeding out employees who are not willing or able to help you move towards your mission. Right now, you are investing in barriers. Paying them is not money well spent. You could be spending the same money on rock stars who would help catapult your progress. Wait until you get to that chapter, or do it now. But know that the weed-out process is coming and must be completed.

In the meantime, at a minimum, please, do not accept defensiveness. Do not feel afraid or walk on eggshells at work. Take baby steps if you must. Do begin to stand up for yourself, your customers, and your mission. Delegate something very small and just walk away. Follow all of the steps in the process. Maybe you will be surprised. If they don't do it, say something. Delegate it again. Begin to give consequences for failure to act. (Again, see the next section, Addressing Your People Problems.)

**Your team does not take responsibility:** You delegate tasks and your employees just shrug their shoulders and say they do not have time. Or, maybe they don't even acknowledge hearing you.

**What it looks like:** Deer in headlights. Everyone looks at you with a blank stare. They have no idea what you are talking about. Or they give you 101 reasons why they couldn't get it done, all with no emotion. They either don't care or don't feel like the task is important.

**What it feels like:** It feels like you are the only one who cares about anything. You have to do it or it won't get done. You are misunderstood or not heard. They have an alternate agenda that you are not aware of that runs contrary to your vision.

**What you can do:** Make sure that you are delegating each task to one specific person. Be especially clear about deadlines and communication timelines to create that call to action. Let them know that they are fully accountable and there are no excuses. If at first you get no response, utilize your discipline process, which is covered later in this book. It won't take long before your team realizes you are serious and there are consequences to a failure to act.

**You are reluctant to give your team more work:** You feel like your team is already too busy. You feel bad for them, so you continue to take on more and more and more. You don't want them to feel overwhelmed or overworked. You want them to like their job. Or, maybe they are really too busy.

**What it looks like:** You are totally stressed out, overworked, and overwhelmed. They are either aware or not. Perhaps they could do more, but think you don't want them to. Or, maybe they don't realize how overworked you are.

**What it feels like:** It feels like you have no time for the work you need to do to lead well. You may feel resentful of your employees because you feel overwhelmed and they have time to relax. You wish they would jump in but they don't.

**What you can do:** Do some reality checking again. Could they take more on? Perhaps their productivity would increase with more work. They may even enjoy the new challenge. If they are actually busy, can you look at some process improvement initiatives? What are you doing that could be done more efficiently? Where can you streamline process? What activities could be minimized or eliminated? Is there anything that could be outsourced? Can you add any additional employees?

**Negative Team attitudes – defensiveness, rudeness, anger, frustration, hostility:** Some negative emotions are legitimate. Maybe you know you aren't a great boss or that the constant need to put out fires has left your team frustrated. You empathize with them. However, even when feelings are legitimate or have an obvious root cause, there is a professional and appropriate way to communicate those feelings.

Other attitudes like defensiveness, rudeness, or hostility, have no place in your business. These are just grown-up versions of temper tantrums used to maintain control. Team members with these attitudes are working to get their way, they are not thinking about your customers.

Your customers are picking up on this negative energy and it is bringing you down. The focus is on the attitudes rather than on the mission.

**What it looks like:** It looks like temper tantrums and immaturity.

**What it feels like:** It feels like terrible negative energy. It feels like power struggles. It feels like poor communication. If your team is getting away with this, one of two scenarios is happening; you are turning a blind eye and trying to avoid it, or are bobbing and weaving to their whims. They would not continue to act this way if it wasn't working.

**What you can do:** You cannot tolerate negative attitudes in your business. Period! Your customers are coming in for your product or service. They do not need a zap of negative energy. And, trust me, they are feeling it or, worse yet, may be experiencing it! Many will not tell you. They will just vote with their feet! Or, perhaps they will tell their friends, "I love my financial planner but I just can't stand the receptionist. She is so rude! It feels like I am an inconvenience when I come in." And, with social media sites like Facebook and Twitter readily available, people can communicate their feelings to a large audience very quickly. Not the kind of press you want for your business!

Now I KNOW this is not the experience you want for your customers. But, reality check time, if you are allowing negative attitudes, this is their experience! Your team is an extension of you, for good or bad. They are a major part of the entire customer experience.

I could go on and on here but will save it for the later chapter when we cover this topic in detail. But this one really gets me!

In the mean time, I will say, be the kind of leader you must be to remove the negativity from your business. When I work with a team exhibiting negative energy I just flat out tell them that it will no longer be tolerated. I teach them about assertive communication. That becomes the new standard. You speak with your mouth, at an appropriate time, with appropriate words, tone, and speed of speech. You use good, positive body language. You respect one another.

When you set out clear expectations for behavior, your team then has a choice to make. They will either choose to act like a grown-up who is focused on your customers or will choose to continue to act like a three-year old. They are empowered to do the right thing or not. It's their choice, their consequence.

Unfortunately, defensive team members find it very difficult to change. A defensive attitude creates a wall that blocks information about change. Often, these team members must go. Give them the opportunity to be successful by clearly communicating the expectation. You can always hire a coach to come in and help you if you need the assistance. Just do something about it. You must!

**You are constantly putting out fires:** You have not taken the time to get ahead of the game. There is no margin in the schedule to allow for planning. Or, you are not organized, so you cannot plan. There is no time to be an effective delegator because you do not think about projects or tasks until you are on top of the deadline. Or, maybe you are an adrenaline junkie who thrives on a deadline. You are subconsciously creating scenarios where you must rush and barely make it.

**What it looks like:** Chaos. Emergencies take priority over day-to-day operation. Then, normal day-to-day operations become an emergency as your team plays catch-up. There is little opportunity to just be. No time to focus on process improvement. You have to bark out orders and hope that things get done. Your team never has the opportunity to prioritize for themselves. The emergencies dictate the timing of your work.

**What it feels like:** Stressful and frustrating! An occasional adrenaline rush can be good, but if you are running like that all the time, you and your team are moving towards burnout. You lose efficiency when you are constantly tugged from one task to another. The prior task is forgotten, or it has to be re-done. You waste time getting re-acclimated. Your rock stars will not want to continue working in that environment; they care too much.

**What you can do:** Are you an adrenaline junky? Is there something in you that enjoys the chaos? Are you artificially creating this environment to feed your need? If so – stop!! Just make an intentional choice to plan ahead. Determine the tasks that your team will take care of, and delegate them well and on time. You can still create some adrenaline rushes for yourself with your own projects, but let them experience some peace!

If it's not you, but your office is this disorganized, then you MUST carve out some time for process improvement. Begin slowly if you must, but start the work. Have your employees begin to think of processes that could work better. Then, as a team, prioritize the list. As I have said before, when I help a team with this, I usually have them start with a few improvements that would be quick fixes with a big impact, the "Big bang for the buck" improvements. Some quick successes will fire your team up to want to do more.

**You do not give clear directions:** Either you are not organized enough yourself to think clearly about what needs to be done, or you are afraid for some reason. By minimizing your requests or using tentative language, you feel like you are cushioning the blow. Maybe you want your team to like you. You are afraid of seeming like a tyrant. If this is your fear, trust me, you are probably far from it.

> **What it looks like:** You provide what you think are clear directions but your team doesn't complete the task. You are not giving any clear call to action. You minimize your delegation with tentative directions like, "When you get to it," or "If you get a chance, can you," or "I was kind of thinking," or "What do you think about," or "Do you think you could?" Okay, you get the picture. None of these statements communicates a sense of urgency. If you are telling them to do it when they get the chance, they may never actually get the chance. If you are asking their opinion, it sounds like they have the option to do it or not, no big deal.

> **What it feels like:** Frustration and confusion. You are frustrated because it feels like your employees aren't listening and never get anything done. They are confused about what they should actually be doing, "Did he mean that we should start using that form now or are we supposed to wait until he tells us to?"

**What you can do:** If organization or clear thought is your issue, own it and get help from a team member who is gifted in that area. Delegate more through a supervisor or office manager, for example. Meet with him or her to communicate what you want done and talk through the steps to getting there. Pass that Olympic Torch to this champion and let them run with it to your team.

If tentative language is your issue, just be very conscious of your word choices. Drop verbiage that waters down your message. You will notice instantly where you are doing it and should be able to easily switch to more powerful, action-provoking phrases. Also, make sure you are communicating those deadlines and communication schedules. A deadline alone can create a call to action.

Sometimes my clients find it helpful to practice saying what they want, or to think through how to say something, in places like their car or when getting ready for the day.

**You are a Tyrant:** Maybe you are overbearing and mean. Perhaps you've been barking orders at your team and then getting openly angry with them when a task is not done to your specifications. Maybe you have good days and bad. On the bad days, you are using your team like human punching bags, hitting them with your words. Delegation under these circumstances will be very difficult because your team members are afraid to take action. They are all trying to hide behind one another. No one wants to be the obvious culprit of the next great offense.

**What it looks like:** Most of the energy in your business is directed at avoiding your wrath. Getting tasks done is secondary. Your customers are secondary. Everyone is walking on eggshells just trying to avoid being the next target. No one wants to stick his or her neck out or take initiative on anything. No one will speak up, that's just like sticking a bull's-eye on your head.

Your attempts at problem solving will all be met with finger pointing and the blame game. The energy will be focused on avoiding the wrath and not fixing the problem. Issues will not be resolved. There is little opportunity for good communication as everyone engages in duck-and-cover, or must match your anger in an attempt to be heard.

**What it feels like:** Negative energy, fear, anxiety, and anger fill your business. At times, some employees may speak back to you, but it will not be in an assertive manner. Some will match your anger in an attempt to be heard. Your customers are feeling it. Some are communicating with their feet.

Honestly, if you are acting like a tyrant, the good team members will not want to work with you for long. Or they will try their hardest and end up with ulcers.

**What you can do:** Get your anger under control. If you need the assistance of a coach or counselor, do it! If you think reading a book will work, do that. You could have the best team in the world but still have negative energy in your facility. You must be your best self to do your important work. You are not being a good steward of your gifts if you are spewing anger. Period.

Nothing your team members are doing justifies your behavior. Sorry! Maybe you have the worst employees in the world. Maybe they cannot do the jobs you have hired them to do. The answer is not to yell like a toddler. The answer is to take the methodical steps spelled out in this book to help them be the right team or get the right employees in and then let them do their jobs.

## Catapult Task: Hurdling the Barriers to Great Delegation

**I have identified these barriers to delegation:**

**My delegation style has this impact on my business or department:**

**My delegation issues have this impact on our customers:**

**I have identified these areas where I could delegate better:**

**I commit to these actions to improve my delegation:**

# Generate Courage to Energize Your Team

*"Success is not final, failure is not fatal: it is the courage
to continue that counts." ~ Winston Churchill*

Remember, the goal is to generate a culture that encourages the energy of unbridled action. We have discussed empowering your employees by providing autonomy to allow for swift response. Unbridled action requires taking some risks. Thus, a second, important variable that allows for unbridled action is a culture that provides a safety net or forgiveness for minor mistakes. In fact, if you could be the kind of leader who encourages mistakes, even better!

See, you can *say* that your team is free to take action without your consent but the reality is, they won't if you have created a culture of fear. If you make your frustration, disappointment, or downright anger known through actions or words when the outcome is not exactly as you would like, your employees will not have the courage to take risks. Through those actions you will generate the belief that mistakes are bad and that employees should follow the prescribed set of work protocols or pay the price.

If you want your employees playing on the small branches, sticking their necks out for your customers and the business, they can not fear getting their head chopped off for a minor infraction. A misstep may warrant a conversation but not a reprimand.

Of course, I am talking about well-intentioned actions to promote business objectives that do not yield an ideal result, not a major infraction resulting from poor choices.

You, as leader, must be intentional about the experiences you create as your employees begin to take risks that are in the best interest of your customers and business. Encourage them by praising them for their efforts. Have conversations about how they could do things differently in the future. Build off each new initiative. Create an environment that fosters courageous action. You don't want a team engaging in duck-and-cover, seeking to be invisible. There is no energy in that!

# Celebrate to Energize Your Team

*"The first responsibility of a leader is to define reality.*
*The last is to say thank you." ~ Max DePree*

Another key to great leadership is to focus on celebration! The best way to keep a room full of people energized and motivated is to have fun with your big adventure. Even serious missions based on helping those in difficult situations are bolstered by a spirit of celebration. Focus on the successes of your team, no matter how small. Remember, what you focus on expands. This is also true for others. Behaviors that get attention tend to show up more often. Employees who are praised for success are much more likely to continue those behaviors that brought the praise.

It becomes easy with the daily grind to lose a sense of what we have accomplished and to fall back into our old habits. The best way to combat this is to actively pursue successes and to publicly celebrate them often. A spirit of celebration keeps the focus on the positive; it reminds you and your team why you are here, in a positive way. By pointing out good things, you are reinforcing those behaviors and values that should be encouraged. You are strengthening every individual's connection to your mission.

I cannot tell you how many times I hear from team members of new clients, "We only hear when there's something wrong. They never tell us when we are doing a good job." It's sometimes difficult to focus on the good when it feels like so much is going awry. But you will burn your team out if you don't provide some positive feedback.

So many leaders I have worked with want to treat appreciation and acknowledgement as if they are limited resources. This does not create a great culture. I often use the analogy of starving people trapped in a room with a few morsels of food. Each person will fight and claw to get what they need. People do the same thing with acknowledgement. One of our innate desires is to be recognized. When we don't receive it, we feel starved.

The truth about gratitude is that the minute you express it, there is another "thank you," ready and available for use. Thank-you's are abundant, share them often.

The goal should be to show plenty of appreciation to all so that no one feels left out. Backbiting, gossip, and sabotage happen when your team sees appreciation as a limited resource. Make recognition abundant, but authentic.

Make a practice of catching your team members doing something good and let them know immediately. You will find plenty of opportunities.

I also recommend beginning a correction with something positive. It is a good rule to make sure the good is staying on your radar. Of course, you do not want that to be the only time you show appreciation. Otherwise, the compliment will automatically signal an imminent reprimand and will no longer feel authentic.

Another great strategy is to schedule individual time with you, either a lunch or a meeting, to give individual employees the time to talk and bond with their leader. Obviously, the size of your team is a factor in how often you can meet individually or whether it's even realistic. If you have a very large team, perhaps you can spend time with one department at a time. Either way, it will give your employees the chance to let you know how they are feeling and what is going on in the business from their perspective. It will also give you one more opportunity to express your gratitude for a job well done.

Here are some ideas for how to celebrate and show your appreciation, some big and some small, some public, some private.

- Pat on the back

- Send a note

- Give praise in a meeting in front of co-workers

- Say, "Great job"

- Say, "I appreciate you"

- Give a thumbs up

- Send an email

- Give a gift card

- Provide a catered lunch

- Use a Wow Board (bulletin board with letters of appreciation from co-workers or customers)

- Let someone choose the office music for the day

- Allow someone an extra hour of sleep

- Give someone a special button to wear for the day or week

- Have a pizza party

- Buy some balloons

- Ask employees what would be meaningful to them

## Encourage Energy Boosting Behavior to Energize Your Team

*"Your first and foremost job as a leader is to take charge of your own energy and then help to orchestrate the energy of those around you." ~ Peter F. Drucker*

Encourage your individual employees to choose high energy. As you'll recall from our earlier discussion of energy, the mood of one person can have an impact on others. Thus, a happy, joyful mood, or a foul, angry mood can each be contagious. Defeating the drama is easier with an energized team. The more energy each individual generates, the better it is for the team and for your customers.

I define energy boosters as people who are positive and upbeat. They leave their life issues at the door and arrive at work ready to focus on your customers. They have a can do attitude and are great team players. Energy busters, on the other hand, have sour moods. They can be whiney and self-centered. They bring their life issues to work and seek support from co-workers for each new self-inflicted challenge they face.

In my team building workshops, I challenge team members to make an intentional choice to be energy boosters, not busters. I encourage you to do the same with your team. It does take effort to hit it everyday, but you can do it and they can too.

Here is a list of qualities to help you determine which of your employees are energy boosters and which are energy busters.

## Energy Busters Exhibit:

✓  Negative Thinking

✓  Victim Mentality

✓  Poor or Aggressive Communication

✓  Gossip

✓  Backstabbing

✓  Focus On Self or Personal Problems

✓  Frustration

✓  Sense of Entitlement

## Energy Boosters Exhibit:

- ✓ Gratitude

- ✓ Focus on Helping Others

- ✓ Positive Thinking

- ✓ Assertive Communication

- ✓ Giving

- ✓ Happiness

- ✓ Teamwork

- ✓ Problem Solving

# Generate Fulfilling Work and a Great Environment to Energize Your Team

*"The more you lose yourself in something bigger than yourself, the more energy you will have." ~ Norman Vincent Peale*

The beauty of this section is, if you have done the work outlined in this book along the way, the result is fulfilling work and a great environment. You have done it or are on your way. This is the end reward for you *AND* your team!

The ultimate is to do work you love. I often say, "My work is play and I love it that way!" My hope is that you will be able to proudly proclaim the same, and mean it!

I hope that you are forging ahead towards making your big vision happen, waking up fired up ready to start your day, that you and your team are fulfilling your business purpose together.

## Catapult Task: Energizing Your Team

**I create these experiences for my team that create fear rather than courage:**

**My team fails to act out of fear or uncertainty in these areas:**

**This failure to act causes these issues with our customers:**

**I commit to encouraging the team to take action in these areas:**

**I will create a safe environment by changing my leadership style in these ways:**

**I commit to focusing on celebration this many times per week:**

**I commit to thanking employees this many times per week:**

**Our team exhibits these energy busting behaviors:**

**I have seen these energy boosting behaviors:**

**I commit to encouraging energy boosting behaviors in these ways:**

**The team is experiencing the gift of fulfilling work in these areas:**

**We still have work to do in these areas to create a great work environment:**

**I commit to improving in these areas to assure that employees are feeling fulfilled:**

# SECTION 3

# Address Your People Problems

*"Talent without discipline is like an octopus on roller skates. There's plenty of movement, but you never know if it's going to be forward, backwards, or sideways." ~ H. Jackson Brown, Jr.*

When my two boys were little we frequented the local fast food play places with friends. It gets cold and snowy during the winter in Michigan so you need a good indoor spot to release little boy energy!

At the end of each play date, the following would occur: I would say, "Come on boys. Time to go." They would stop what they were doing immediately, walk directly to me and say, "Thank you for bringing me Mommy."

Jaws dropped and eyes popped in amazement. I often had moms ask, "How did you get them to do that?"

My secret: I set the expectations up front and told them the consequences. And the third, most important variable to achieving the jaw-dropping response, my boys needed to know through experience that I was the kind of mom who would follow through.

What the other parents didn't see is that before leaving the car we went through this exercise without fail:

I would ask my two boys, "What are the rules?"

And they would repeat the following:

"I have to finish eating my lunch before I play."
"Very good. What else?"
"I have to play nice the entire time."
"Absolutely. What else?"
"I can't whine or complain when it's time to go."
"Perfect. And?"
"When you say it's time to leave I have to run to you and say, 'thank you for bringing me mommy"
"Perfect! And if these four things don't happen. What is the consequence?
"I can't come back for a really long time."

And I was a mom who followed through with consequences, so they were not going to chance it. Now it is time to arm you with the tools to be the kind of leader who will follow through if you haven't in the past.

In the previous section, we talked about many strategies for communicating clear expectations. Now we need to add the action to take if an employee has the opportunity to be successful, but does not choose well.

By this point, you have given your individual team members plenty of opportunities to exhibit their excitement and passion about your mission and they should be starting to align. Based on the Catapult Task you completed, you should have a clear understanding of where each employee excels and struggles in terms of their knowledge, skills, abilities, and personality. Hopefully, you have communicated with your team members and implemented some strategies to address shortfalls among solid team members and have been providing plenty of opportunities to participate with you on your journey to success.

However, my guess is, some things still aren't quite right. You are still being blindsided here and there. Because, unfortunately, the tough work is not quite done. As I've said before, I do believe that most employees want to do a good job. However, there will be some who are not able or willing to do the work required to be successful. They are not interested in being fueled, focused, and fired up. Instead, they prefer to use their creative energy to avoid participating and to work in whatever way suits them.

This section, Addressing Your People Problems, is a key step to defeating the drama. If you thought you'd be able to tolerate bad behavior and still achieve a drama-free zone, you, unfortunately, are not accurate.

The reality is, if you are tolerating less than optimal behavior, you will still have drama, period. If you allow employees to break your flow, you are losing efficiency, failing your customers, frustrating your rock stars, and generating drama. A conflict between two employees rarely affects just the two involved. Regardless of the cause, drama between employees creates what I call collateral damage.

You may already know this all too well, but in case you've tried to avoid looking at the big picture, let's dive in. So, two employees do not get along. You have the lost productivity from any time they spend arguing rather than working. In addition, there is lost work time from one avoiding a task that includes the other.

Meanwhile, the rest of the team may avoid contact or waste time listening to the complaints. And let's not forget the built up resentments from those who are picking up the slack for the resulting lost productivity.

I once worked with a team that included a very cantankerous receptionist. In my brief time there, I heard many stories about the negative impact her attitude had on customer service beyond the obvious, a less than friendly face at the front door! Employees avoided asking the receptionist for the information they needed to do their jobs. Moreover, they did not want to enter her area to gather the information themselves, for fear of angering her. This resulted in frequently delayed customer orders.

In another organization, two employees did not get along and asked to be scheduled apart. The manager was constantly jumping through hoops to create a schedule that worked for them, often to the detriment of customer service. And the accommodation didn't make the drama go away. The two still complained about each other incessantly and no amount of accommodation was ever enough. As you can probably guess, this caused drama.

When certain individuals are engaging in activities that take them away from work, the employees who pick up the slack become resentful. Generally, these are your rock star employees. The ones you want to keep happy, so they continue working for you.

You, as leader, may end up losing productive time mediating conversations between the two. Or, perhaps disgruntled co-workers approach you to complain or ask you to problem solve.

The team dynamic as a whole will suffer. Some will take sides; while other employees will do all they can to steer clear. Either way, it is energy focused on activities other than serving your customers. And this, as you now know well, is a recipe for drama.

Even if you have 125 employees aligned with mission, they will still harbor resentment towards the one who is skating by. There will be lost productivity. Again, think back to the credit union example. It is quite possible that entire dynamic resulted from leadership tolerance of one employee who sought to avoid customer contact.

Should I continue? I know you know this already, but you may be in denial. I want you to develop a yearning to address your people problems.

Get real. Think about the last time there was drama in your business. What was the issue? What was the result? Try to think of *all* the consequences rather than just the most obvious. What was your response? Did you engage in duck-and-cover? Did you try to help fix it, or did you encourage your team to find a solution? Did you work towards creating a culture that doesn't tolerate drama, or did you fuel the fire by putting extra focus and energy there, giving the drama seekers time and attention?

You can demand no more from any one employee than you do from your lowest performing employee.

Stop and think about that for a minute. Picture your most difficult employee. How much drama do they create? How many excuses do they give? How ineffective are they?

Now, picture every team member functioning at that same level. Every time I do this presentation, I get a laugh during this section. Not a belly laugh, mind you. More of an, "oh no" chuckle. It is almost universal. At least one employee always easily comes to mind.

Really, visualize:

- What would your business be like?

- How would it function?

- What would it feel like for your customers?

- Would your billing get done?

- Would orders get filled correctly and efficiently?

- What kind of quality would you provide?

- Would your phone get answered?

- Would customer information be up to date?

- What kind of energy would you have in your business?

Your other employees are accommodating the performance you allow from that individual. They are working harder, picking up slack, dealing with unnecessary drama, trying to protect your customers, and trying to protect you. And they are building up resentment.

If it is really bad, your great employees will get burned-out and decide to go elsewhere. You will be left with that poor performer who has fewer options. If this is your circumstance, those satisfied with the drama and chaos are happy because it is working for them!

You cannot tolerate anything less than excellence! You have important work to do and you need top-notch employees to help you get there. Your team is an extension of you! How many customers have you lost due to rude treatment from an employee? That credit union lost two in a day. Or how many of your customers are barely tolerating the treatment because they feel such loyalty to you, your service or product. This is not what you want for your customers!

You want your customers to have an excellent experience with you from start to finish. Fill your business with the right kind of employees and good processes, and they will.

You cannot defeat the drama with dead weight. Most, if not all, of my clients have at least one employee who is not a right fit. We start by transforming the leadership style, making sure that everyone has the opportunity to be successful, and, inevitably, there is at least one person who thinks they will be able to continue to behave the way they have all along. They are usually the victim person, or the "Life is Hard Sympathy Card" employee that we'll discuss shortly. They often claim their employers are, "just out to get me." They use all kinds of defense mechanisms to stay exactly as they are, and instead try to change the world around them to meet their own needs.

If you have one or more of these people in your business, they have to go. Your other team members will grow, learn, transform, and work hard to establish a new culture and improved energy. This employee will do everything in his or her power to sabotage those efforts. There is always collateral damage when you have a team member who does not wish to do the right thing. If they are unproductive, they are not just stealing work hours; they are creating resentment in your other employees.

It is a privilege to work for you, not an entitlement or a right. If they have financial needs, it is not up to you to give them the means to fulfill their obligations. It is up to them. A self-actualized person who needs money will make the right choices to keep their job. They will not look to others to create an environment that suits them to keep a position. There is no guilt here. Each employee has free will. If you are doing everything in your power to allow them the opportunity to be successful and they are still choosing to fail, it is their choice, their doing. Release them out into the world to find a work environment that better fits who they want to be on the job. They will be happier in the end, and so will your team.

## Catapult Task: Analyzing the Impact of My Accommodations

Let's get clear on the full impact your accommodations are having on your business, team, and customers. I bet you haven't taken the time to sit down and pull it all together. Are you ready? It may be much bigger than you think. It's a necessary exercise though. Seeing the full impact in one spot will help create the motivation you need to change. You know what they say, "The pain of staying the same has to be worse than the pain of the change."

Let's create enough pain to motivate you through the fear of some team members being unhappy, angry, upset, sad, or throwing temper tantrums.

**I am making these accommodations for poor performers:**

**These accommodations are having this impact on my business:**

**These accommodations are having this impact on my team:**

**These accommodations are having this impact on my rock star employees:**

**These accommodations are having this impact on my customers:**

**These accommodations are having this impact on the employee I am making them for:**

**I will maintain appropriate standards and allow my team to choose freely. I commit to making these changes without guilt:**

◡◠

# The ABC's of Addressing Your People Problems

*"We are free to choose our paths, but we can't choose the consequences that come with them." ~ Sean Covey*

In the last section, you evaluated your employees and determined whether each had the key basic ingredients for success, the willingness, and the ability; and you should have developed a plan for any who were lacking. Did you begin having the conversations with your team? If you haven't already, now is time to start the sometime tough work of communicating the need for change and following up with those who have failed to comply. You must have the conversations necessary to put the plans in action. Begin communicating clearly and allow those individuals to decide if they will stay with you or not. Will they help the organization achieve or will they continue to be a source of drama?

Nothing matters more than the success of your business. It is time to go to the mat for you, your customers, and your team. As always, no need to worry if you are feeling uncertain or ill-prepared. We will arm you with the tools you need to achieve success.

I call these next steps the ABC's of Addressing Your People Problems. We will cover:

- **A**djust your mindset and get into **A**ction

- **B**ust the 4 D's of Discipline Avoidance

- **C**onsistency

# Adjust Your Mindset: Create the Courage for Quality Correction Conversations

*"Trust is knowing that when a team member does push you, they're doing it because they care about the team." ~ Patrick Lencioni*

The truth is, all my clients know that they *should* be doing something to address their people problems. They know they should not tolerate bad behavior or poor performance.

It is always one or both of these barriers that stand in the way:

Fear or guilt that stops you in your tracks. You have not created a mindset that empowers you to address your people problems well. The most common fears and false beliefs that I hear are:

- They Might be Angry or Defensive

- They Have So Much Going On

- I don't Know How to Start

- It Doesn't Make a Difference Anyway

- They Might Quit

- They're My (fill in blank) Aunt, Neighbor, Cousin, Best Friend's Sister.

You are not sure how to have a correction conversation.

- How do you start?

- What do you say?

- What do you document?

- What if they get angry?

I get it, it is difficult to have a correction conversation with an employee. Most are not jumping for joy at the prospect of sitting down with you to have the conversation. As a matter of fact, there seems to be a negative correlation between the need for correction and the attitude; the higher the need the worse the attitude, right?

And if you've avoided having these conversations for a long time, the situation is even worse. You are less confident and your employees are more accustomed to doing their own thing. It's working for them, especially those who are entitled and use every ounce of their creativity to avoid work.

So, let's start by arming you with the two most important tools to address your people problems and defeat the drama!

First, let's work to adjust your mindset.

I find that even my clients who know what to do, often do not follow through. Almost always, it boils down to a mindset that keeps them from utilizing the policy well. Many of my clients have fear and guilt about holding employees accountability and following through with consequences. It is like buying the gym membership but never using it. You know that you are supposed to work out, but you have stuff in the way.

- You haven't carved out the time

- You haven't pulled your exercise clothes together

- You fear what people will think of you when they see you in your workout clothes

- You don't know how to use some of the equipment and fear looking silly

And on and on it goes.

My clients are just as good at justifying their inability to have correction conversations. They know they need to do them, but they

- Haven't carved out the time

- Aren't really familiar with the forms or how to use them

- Fear what the employee will think of them or how he or she might respond

- Worry that the employee needs the job and don't want to jeopardize their employment,

- Fear losing the skills of an employee – and on and on

If I am describing you, let's adjust your mindset so you can generate successful correction conversation. Believe it or not, it often takes just a minor mindset tweak to move from fear and guilt to courage and action.

When you are having a correction conversation with an employee, it is an investment in their success. You are giving them one-on-one, personalized time to make sure they understand what is required to be successful. It is a time to problem-solve, create commitments to each other, and hopefully to salvage their employment.

Ultimately, you are on their side. You want them to be successful. Communicating assertively provides the clarity and focus they need for the opportunity to succeed. Without the conversation, it is possible that your employee was not clear about what was expected, and instead was living in assumption. A good correction conversation yields clarification and documentation of what is required to achieve excellence.

Focusing on your own fear or guilt changes your non-verbal communication. Instead, focus on the following statements to empower yourself and communicate boldly, courageously, and confidently:

- I want you to be successful

- I will define what success is

- I will communicate the definition to you

- You will have a choice

- I hope you choose well

The message of this mindset is that you, as the leader, will define what success is, not the employee. You will communicate that definition. The employee then has the free will to choose to act differently based on the new information, or continue down the same path. The final step is that you hope they make the right choice so you don't have to do what you'd rather not. However, you won't put your business at risk to save their job. There is no guilt, because once you communicate clear expectations, the employee is the one with the power to choose success. The ball is in their court.

A few years ago, I worked with a business where a long-term employee was about to be terminated and the manager was wracked with guilt. The employee was an x-ray tech and had let her certification lapse. This was obviously a huge liability issue for the business. The manager had given her 2 *years* (yes, you are reading that right, years) to do what she needed to do to renew the certification and had offered to pay for the classes.

The employee chose to do nothing, took not one class. Instead, she chose to spend her time and energy walking around telling everyone how her employer was trying to push her out of her job.

- Was every effort made to help this employee? Yes.

- Did the employee have final control over taking the classes or not? Yes.

- Who is at fault for the termination? The employee.

- Is it reasonable for a business to take on the liability of utilizing an uncertified x-ray tech to accommodate this team member's desire to continue with status quo? No!

- Is it acceptable for her to rile up the other team members with her denial? No!

- Should the manager feel guilty? No!

*Do not take on guilt where you have no control.*

You cannot control other people's actions and you cannot control their perceptions. They will have their own life experience and you need to allow that. Sometimes their perceptions will cause them to be angry with you; you have to be okay with that. Sometimes those perceptions are the defense mechanism that keeps them stuck where they are. They are using their flawed perception to feel like a victim. A victim is unable to take action or make change. They don't want to take ownership of their own lives, so they need to place blame on someone else. At times, that someone might be you. Let them blame, but do not take it on as guilt!

Now, being okay with their anger is not the same as being okay with them acting out because of that anger. Being okay with their anger is not letting your fear of their anger stop you from holding them to reasonable standards, regardless of their circumstance. You are absolutely allowed and encouraged to stop them from acting out as a result of their anger. It's about setting boundaries and sticking to them. An employee can be angry about being held accountable, but they cannot act out because of that anger. They need to act professionally and appropriately. Do not tolerate storming, stomping, throwing, slamming, eye rolling, yelling, swearing, or anything resembling these actions. There are more consequences if a team member cannot act professionally. Period. (We will be talking about these consequences in subsequent chapters).

You set the standard for this too. They can then choose to act appropriately or not. If they have a lot of bad stuff going on in their lives and really need the job, then they'd better make the right choice. They may not. It's their choice. No guilt.

Got it?

## Catapult Task: Generating the Courage for Quality Correction Conversations

**These fears currently stop me from having productive correction conversations:**


**I have taken on guilt in these areas:**


**I am creating an opportunity for success in these ways when I have quality correction conversations:**


**This is in my control when I have a correction conversation:**


**This area is not in my control when I have a correction conversation:**


**I gain this when I have quality correction conversations:**


**Our customers gain this when I have quality correction conversations:**

**Our team members gain this when I have a quality correction conversation:**

⌒◦◦⌒

# Get In Action

*"An ounce of action is worth a ton of theory."*
*~ Ralph Waldo Emerson*

Adjust your mindset, and then get into action. No longer let your justifications keep you silent.

Let's take a further look at the X-ray Tech example. If that leader had addressed the situation with this new mindset, might the outcome have been different? While we can't know for sure, one thing is certain, that employee would have been less inclined to stick with her defense that the mean employer was trying to push her out of her job. Rather than lending a sympathetic ear, the leader may have addressed the situation by:

- Being more assertive and urging the tech to do what was required to save her job

- Having the frank conversation that more accurately illustrated the facts

- Communicating that the employee actually had the ultimate power to save her own job

- Communicating that while it required action the employee was not happy with, this was the definition of success. Now choose.

This did not happen. Instead the leader avoided the topic, did not get in action. The leader never pushed back, and perhaps left the tech with the deluded assumption that she might keep her job based on her own criteria. Dodging the conversation for two years did nothing to promote action. While we can't predict whether a quality correction conversation would have given the tech the call to action she needed, it would have given her an improved potential for success.

Your intent is not to hurt your employees. On the contrary, your intent is to help them by giving them every opportunity to be successful. Staying silent provides no advantage to the employee or the business in the long run. Have the courage to do what you must.

## Catapult Task: Get in Action

It's time to practice your new mindset and get in action. If you haven't done it already, pull out the KSAP analysis you did with your individual team members in the last section and get communicating. Each employee deserves to know where he or she stands. You or one of your leaders must sit down with each employee individually to share where they are and any required steps they must take to achieve success.

## Get in Action with Defined Consequences: The Tools of Great Accountability

A key ingredient in the formula for defeating drama and connecting with your customers is accountability. To create accountability, you need clear expectations and consistent follow-through on objective consequences. Similar to taking kids to a fast food play place, establish the consequences up-front and then follow through consistently where necessary.

This does not mean taking your discipline to the extreme and creating a culture of fear; you are just looking for opportunities to assert yourself.

You don't want your employees to feel like you are standing over them with a hammer ready to swat if they make the tiniest mistake. But you can't have them dictating what happens in your business each day, either. You must be a leader who follows through on a promise to act.

Give clear directions utilizing your great delegation techniques, provide your team with the tools needed, and if they consistently fail to follow your instructions, follow through as promised. While I believe most people want to do a good job, there are times when employees fall short. Some employees need a little external motivation to achieve excellence. Still others just cannot seem to get it at all. For these circumstances, there must be consequences spelled out up-front. These tools shouldn't be used each time you delegate. They are tools in your tool belt during your day-to-day operation.

With the right team, you will need to use these tools only occasionally. However, if you see that a tough transition is required, you or your designate may be using these tools quite a bit initially.

The first and most important tool in your tool belt is the Progressive Discipline Process.

## Get in Action with a Progressive Discipline Process

A good discipline process includes the consequences of inappropriate behavior, written in detail, and allows for consistency. It is titled progressive discipline because the consequences outlined become progressively worse.

I've had clients who had no established discipline process when I started with them.

They would either:

- Do nothing to address issues

- Speak to employees but provide no consequences when employees don't follow through

- Or use the hunt-and-peck approach to discipline, coming up with new consequences randomly on the fly.

I remember one client in particular. As I worked with one of the owners to transform his leadership, he would share the highlights of his previous week. Often the updates included issues he had with employees. "This employee did X so I sent him home for the rest of the day."

Then about another incident I'd hear, "I'm docking his pay." Still another, "I made her stay late and do work she hates."

Each time I would cringe, share my thoughts, and once again recommend a solid discipline process with outlined consequences.

You see, there were telling outcomes from his stories. One, there was no consistency to his consequences, that is the most obvious; but the second and probably more important, employees were always doing things that required discipline! What he was doing was not working!

There was no rhyme or reason, no logic, no aligning the consequence with the severity of the offense. Not only are random consequences ineffective, they can get you into legal trouble.

The goal of a good discipline process is to have a team that rarely requires its use. A good discipline process will effectively transform a dysfunctional team, so it is rarely required after the initial stage.

To me, the discipline process is something in your tool belt that you need only seldom. Once your employees realize you follow through with consequences, they will follow the rules. Most do not want to be written up or lose their jobs. If you implement a discipline process and they do not care, you do not have the right team. No problem. Just take them through the process and get them exited out. Win – Win, either way!

Trust me; your rock stars love a great discipline process. It will keep the other employees in line. They can start to see a light at the end of the tunnel as you move a problem employee towards termination.

If someone is complaining about the process, he or she is trying to find a way around your rules.

Consult with a professional if you need assistance. This may not be your forte and that is okay. Others have strengths in this area. Utilize them to get you set up. Better to get the right tools in place than to let something simple stop you.

## Recommendations for a Progressive Discipline Process

Some infractions are more serious than others. In general, violations that are more serious will result in more serious disciplinary action. Based on that premise, I recommend dividing the work rules in to two groups:

- **Group I Violations:** are less serious in nature. Violations will result in the progressive disciplinary steps described in this section.

- **Group II Violations:** are considered very serious and any violation will generally result in immediate discharge or at least some time off without pay.

## The Four Levels of Disciplinary Action

### Corrective Action Notice
A Corrective Action Notice should be issued for a first violation of a Group I work rule. At this step, the supervisor should tell the employee exactly what offense has been committed and outline the proper action that must be followed to correct the situation. The

employee is encouraged to explain his/her actions. The employee should also be asked to sign a copy of the Corrective Action Notice to indicate that he/she has read it. The notice becomes a part of the employee's file. If there is no further discipline within a 12-month period, the notice will no longer be considered for the purpose of progressive discipline.

## First-Level Written Warning

A first–level written warning is given if the employee has committed what could be considered a Group I rule violation and has previously received a Corrective Action Notice for a Group I rule violation within the last 12 months. A written warning details the offense and the policy involved. If the employee disagrees with any of the facts, he/she should have the opportunity to add a statement to the record. Again, the employee should be asked to sign a copy of the warning to indicate that he/ she has read it. This warning becomes a part of the employee's record. If no further offenses occur within a 12-month period, the warning will no longer be considered for the purpose of progressive discipline.

## Second-Level Written Warning

A second-level written warning should be issued for any violation if an employee has received a first-level written warning within the last 12 months. Or, if the employee has engaged in activity that falls under a Group II violation. At this level, a one- to-five day suspension without pay, may accompany a written warning for violations other than absenteeism or tardiness.

### Third-Level Written Warning

Receiving a third-level written warning for any violation within a 12-month period should be cause for discharge if the employee has two active written warnings. You may also go straight to a Third-Level Written Warning if the offense is especially egregious. In either case, the third written warning should result in termination of employment.

## Catapult Task: Discipline Process

**We fall short in these areas with our current discipline process:**

**I commit to creating and rolling out a discipline process for my organization or using the one we have:**

**I commit to following up with discipline when it is appropriate:**

**I commit to holding my team accountable to the high standards that will help us achieve excellence and great service:**

# Busting the 4 D's of Discipline Avoidance

*"A 'No' uttered from the deepest conviction is better
than a 'Yes' merely uttered to please, or worse,
to avoid trouble." ~ Mohandas Ghandi*

Now that you've created a new mindset, let's walk through the steps to generating a successful correction conversation.

Defeating the drama and generating a dynamic team requires great communication, both of expectations and of issues. Most employees will respond well to correction. They will appreciate the feedback, take it to heart, and make the required changes. After all, you are providing them with a clear definition of success and a path to get there. They are on sound footing, knowing where they stand.

Some employees, however, have no desire to change and will do whatever it takes to remain stuck where they are. I will term these employees, "problem employees." These are the team members who probably do not belong and will ultimately be walked through your discipline process and out the door, if you choose to follow through.

Problem employees will often use tactics to avoid owning their bad behavior. They are stuck in a rut and have no desire to change. I have identified four groups of common avoidance strategies that I call the 4 D's of Discipline Avoidance. They are:

- **Deflection:** High jacking the conversation to avoid the conversation about their own issues.

- **Denial:** Utilizing one's creative capacity to refute any evidence that supports they have done anything wrong.

- **Defensiveness:** An aggressive tactic to quiet the leader.

- **Defriending:** Brings back images of 7th grade when ostracizing a fellow student was used as a punishment.

When faced with these tactics, leaders are often paralyzed by fear. They adopt a keep-quiet approach, which hurts the entire team by robbing everyone the opportunity for constructive feedback.

That, obviously, is not the best strategy. Instead, let's arm you with some tools to bust the 4 D's of discipline avoidance so you can move forward with the communication that must happen for your team to excel.

Remember the keys to your new mindset. You may want to print the list and have them in front of you. This mindset will help keep you calm and will drive your non-verbal communication. Here they are again for a refresher:

- I want you to be successful

- I will define what success is

- I will communicate the definition to you

- You will have a choice

- I hope you choose well

The goal during the entire meeting is for you to remain calm, communicate what you must, and maintain control. Do not allow the employee to hijack the meeting and use the tactics below to avoid escalation.

As you begin the meeting, ask the employee to listen until you are finished and tell them that they will have a chance to speak after you are through. Throughout the conversation, continue to emphasize that you want them to be successful and that you hope they will make the right choices. This communicates to them that they are empowered to do what's right. There is no one else to blame. This will help reinforce the concept for you as well, in case you are feeling guilty unnecessarily.

Keep the entire meeting short and sweet. Stick to the point. If he or she attempts to highjack the meeting, do not allow it. We'll be covering the specific strategies to use shortly.

When you are through, have the employee sign the form. They may add a few written comments if they wish.

Needless to say, their reaction during the meeting usually gives you a good indication of whether they are going to make the necessary changes to be successful going forward. Ideally, the discipline is a wakeup call. They will see that you are serious and will choose to alter their behavior to keep their job. If not, just keep walking them through the discipline process until they are out the door.

Here are some specific strategies to adopt to help you achieve your goal of maintaining control of the correction conversation as employees use the most popular avoidance techniques.

# Deflection

An employee utilizing this tactic will bring up everything under the sun to highjack the meeting. Their goal is to change the topic and move the conversation away from them. You'll hear about all the wrong doings of your management team, fellow employees, and systems. You may hear about issues going on in their lives. Do not fall prey.

Following them down the rabbit trails will just leave both of you confused. You will run out of time before you get to the topic you intended. The employee will leave feeling like, "phew, bought myself more time." And the same behavior will continue.

Stick to your agenda no matter what. They may get more and more creative as the meeting progresses. Stick to your guns. Your number one goal is to maintain control of the meeting and stick to the topic. If they do happen upon an issue that deserves further investigation, jot it down as an action item to tackle after the meeting, and move on.

Use phrases like these:

- "We are not here to discuss that right now. We are here to talk about you."

- "That is not your concern. I need you to focus on your own issues and the changes you must make to be successful."

- "I understand that that must be difficult for you. I encourage you to speak to a professional about that. In the mean time, let's focus on your work here."

# Denial

Some employees will vehemently deny responsibility when the hard evidence is sitting right in front of them. It does not matter. You may not ever convince them or get them to own up. And, unfortunately, that is the first step required for them to make real change. Most who adopt this avoidance technique will not be successful. Use phrases like these:

- "I am concerned that you are not able to take responsibility. If you are unwilling to acknowledge you were in error I feel that you will not make the changes required to be successful."

- "I am not here to debate what happened. I am here to talk about next steps with you based on what did happen."

- "You will have an opportunity to speak briefly and add your comments to the form at the end. For now I need you to listen to me."

# Defensiveness

Employees will vary in the degree to which they will defend themselves and at times can become quite angry. The fear of this response is one that stops many of my clients. However, you can not relinquish control by letting fear stop you. In this instance you must maintain control of the meeting. Do not allow them to escalate. Use phrases like:

- "I need you to use a softer tone."

- "Please watch your language."

- "You must decrease the volume of your voice."

- "I need you to calm down and listen."

- "This is not appropriate behavior."

Speak at a normal pace and use soft tones. Try not to match their volume. This can help bring them back down. Continue to be encouraging. Let them know that you are hoping that they will make the right choice and will be successful.

- "I want you to be successful. I am hoping that you hear me today and make the right choices going forward."

- "I need you to stop and listen because I really want you to get this one now."

- "Your success begins with you listening to me and actually hearing what I am saying to you."

## De-Friending

Yes, sometimes the people who report to you won't like you. They must treat you with respect. They must do their jobs, but they don't have to like or agree with everything you do, and that has to be okay with you. Period. Please don't let the fear of their disapproval cause you to give away power to your team.

If an employee begins hurling threats that remind you of high school, combat them with phrases like these:

- "I am sorry to hear that. I will continue to respect you and really do hope that you do what is necessary to be successful."

- "This is not personal. It is about the job. I really hope that you hear what I say today and make the right choices."

**Outcome:** Either you get a transformed employee who realizes that they no longer have the power to dictate the culture of your organization or that employee is no longer there wreaking havoc. Either way you win! Additionally, other employees will see that you are serious and will be less apt to test the waters.

Documentation, in either case, is important. It provides a good tool for communicating clear expectations, but you have also created a paper trail that evidences your attempts at helping your employee be successful. Often my clients fear the repercussions of a lawsuit. Those fears are not without merit. I always say that you can not stop someone from filing suit you can only prepare yourself in case it happens. Frivolous lawsuits do happen after a termination but most former employees do not take that action. So, just make sure that you have documentation. Even unemployment claims can be thwarted with good documentation. Do not let fear stop you here. What cost are you incurring by keeping poor performers on board? Remember, it is not just the lost productivity from these individuals but also the collateral damage they create within your business and amongst the other team.

Remember, you can always call on a trusted advisor with human resource expertise if you feel uncertain.

## Catapult Task: Busting the 4 D's of Discipline Avoidance

**I have experienced these avoidance tactics from my team members:**

**My response had this affect on our team and customers:**

**I commit to responding this way in the future:**

# Consistency

*"There is no use whatever trying to help people who do not help themselves. You cannot push anyone up a ladder unless he be willing to climb himself." ~ Andrew Carnegie*

The key is to follow the process when you have employee issues. It does you no good to have a discipline process sitting in a binder getting dusty. And you must follow it consistently. You cannot play favorites. If you have family members on your team, they cannot be exempt. That sets a very poor example and will lead to all kinds of drama.

At times my clients find it easier to correct their high performers. They are always up for some good constructive feedback. Overtime, however, this breeds resentment. They begin to realize that the poor performers are not being held to the same standards and are rarely spoken to.

Keep the 4 D's of Discipline Avoidance handy. These strategies will help you follow through with employees who are more difficult to speak with.

I'll go back to the example of the client I had who pulled consequences out of thin air on the fly. His tactics did not work. The employees looked at the discipline as a knee jerk reaction to an event. His consequences did nothing to shepherd their behavior towards a specified, better behavior and did a lot towards generating drama.

It is often difficult to apply consequences consistently. We have empathy for some employees because of their situations. The goal is not to become legalistic or dictatorial. I encourage you to apply some logic. For instance, if one of your team members pulled an all-nighter to complete an important project for a customer, be flexible on that tardiness policy.

If you find, however, that an individual's personal circumstances are causing you to work around company policy often, then that is a red flag that warrants a closer look.

The employee who is in constant turmoil can sometimes inspire us to do a lot of accommodating. This is not where you want to generate wiggle room, however. You are working too hard to defeat the drama to become the source now.

Think back to the visualization we did earlier. You cannot apply higher standards to any one employee than you do to your lowest performer without generating new drama.

A particular challenge is maintaining this empowered mindset with what I call the "Life is Hard Sympathy Card" Employee. Leaders in the helping professions, in particular, fall prey to this one easily and allow their team to play the hand too often. That heart to serve makes you want to save the world and help your employees at every turn. You are wracked with guilt if you do not do all that you can for someone. Unfortunately, often what I've seen is that it goes too far. You do not want to be an enabler. And, in particular, you don't want to put your business at risk to accommodate employees who are playing the "Life is Hard Sympathy Card".

They wreak havoc in your business by coming to work crying and whining about the latest crisis in their lives. They pull all of the focus onto themselves. You'd love to have these team members and the rest of your team focus some of their energy on your customers but you feel so bad for them. Maybe this time they'll get it together. You allow them to be unproductive, give them extra time off, and ignore their tardiness. Maybe you listen to their problems too, but at a minimum allow other team members time away from work to lend an ear. I even had one client give a "Life is Hard Sympathy Card" employee a big bonus every year to try to help. She was a single mom struggling through one self-inflicted crisis after another. The result was no change in behavior, no appreciation, no productivity, just a sense of entitlement and anger when the bonuses stopped.

The problem is that, more often than not, it's the employee's choices that are putting them in these bad situations and work is not the place to go for sympathy and support. Yes, of course we can care about one another. This isn't about being a cold fish and turning off your heart. However, at work, the focus needs to be on customers. If these employees have no time or energy left for your customers, over an extended period, they need to go to a place where it is appropriate to talk about their issues, where they can get the support and professional assistance they need to change. They don't need a shoulder to cry on as they repeat the same patterns over and over.

Many times the employees using the 'Life is Hard Sympathy Card' are allowed to behave with complete disregard to those around them because your servant's heart makes you feel guilt if you cannot help. You can't discipline or terminate them because you feel bad for them; they need the job.

Here are just some of the reasons I've heard for not holding someone accountable - repeatedly, I might add:

- His family won't have anything to do with him.

- She's a single mom. She really needs this job.

- Her husband is an alcoholic.

- He's filing for bankruptcy.

- She's been having issues with an abusive boyfriend.

- Her kids have been getting into trouble at school.

- They are in foreclosure.

- His wages are being garnished.

- He has nowhere else to turn.

- She's really upset because her boyfriend is cheating on her.

Is all of this tough stuff? Yep. Do you think it's possible that some of your rock star employees have gone through some of this as well but chose to be professional and put their problems aside while at work? It isn't a requirement to share your personal dramas at work. But, it's serving some of your employees well if you continue to accommodate them as a result.

Those using the "Life is Hard Sympathy Card" need to want the job as bad as you want them to have the job. If they really need it, they need to make the right choices to keep it. You can't keep accommodating their choices by making the job convenient for them because you fear the thought of them losing their income.

They don't get to set the bar for behavior, energy, and productivity in your business; you do. What level of performance do they need to maintain to keep the job that they need so terribly? Where does their focus need to be? If they really want the job, they will rise to the occasion and do what they need to do to keep it.

If they don't make the right choice there should be no guilt. They are given a choice. Here's the standard of work required; now choose. Your team members have the free will to choose to do what they need to do to keep the job or not. It is your job to clearly communicate these requirements.

If your fear makes you waiver and change your expectations of a team member, you are allowing another person to dictate the culture and direction of your business, tolerating workplace drama that is impacting your bottom line. Their choices have put their life in shambles. Do you really want them dictating *anything* that happens in your workplace? Is this really what you want?

## Catapult Task: Addressing Your People Problems

I have been inconsistent in addressing my people problems in these areas (speaking more freely with high performers, being more lenient with defensive employees, giving preferential treatment to family, friends or others on the team):

I commit to continuing to assure that team members are meeting the standards that I set:

I concede that these employees do not fit with the remarkable team that I am creating:

My customers, business, and team are suffering these consequences as a result:

I commit to the following actions to address these shortfalls to provide these employees with an opportunity to be successful if they make the right choices:

# SECTION 4

# Defeat the Drama with a Dynamic Team

*"In the end, all business operations can be reduced to three words: people, product and profits. Unless you've got a good team, you can't do much with the other two." ~ Lee Iacocca*

This is it! You are in the last section! You have achieved fuel, focus, and fire as a leader, have engaged and empowered your team, and have addressed your people problems. The last and final phase of defeating the drama is bringing those high powered, fired up individuals together as a team that is fueled for the business mission, empowered to take action in a focused way, and fired up! Each individual must know his or her part in the mission and how it fits with the rest of the team or other departments. They must all play nice together. This is the last phase of creating a harmonious work environment.

Now it is time to organize this group of individuals into a team. The final phase of defeating the drama is about making sure that your team is coordinated and committed to each other and your customers. It is time to design the way they work together.

This final phase should be a simple one. Each person is fueled, focused, and fired up. They have the resources they need to be successful. Now we need to eliminate the opportunity for unhealthy competition or petty disagreements.

Ultimately, our relationships are created through communication. It is how we bond as human beings. Communication amongst your team members will be key. It is time to create team commitments for how they will communicate, work together, what they will assume about one another, and how they will maintain the positive flow and focus that you have achieved through your work thus far.

# Defeat the Drama with Good Team Communication

*"The void created by the failure to communicate is soon filled with poison, drivel and misrepresentation." ~ C. Northcote Parkinsin*

Good communication is the key to any healthy relationship. Even people in healthy relationships have disagreements periodically. It is a normal part of human interaction. Seeing some healthy conflict means that your team is engaged in your business and feels confident enough to speak up. This is a good thing. A silent meeting is the sign of an unhealthy team. Employees are afraid to speak up, are harboring resentments with each other, do not trust one another, or just do not care enough to exert the effort to design or voice an opinion. If you experience this in your team meetings, I guarantee you are suffering from drama.

Encourage healthy discussions and debates. You want everyone to have a voice. You never know where that next great idea might come from.

And when there is a conflict, encourage your team members to work out their differences themselves wherever possible. If a grievance is worth spending any time on, it should be productive time used to improve the situation rather than just for gossiping, complaining, and creating drama.

Pull yourself and everyone else out of the mediator role. Think how much time that wastes! Focusing time on petty disagreements and hurts, just sends the message that it's okay to engage in them, and gives the impression that you will tolerate drama. You can end up with employees pitting themselves against one another or vying for your attention with protests.

If you have been at the center of many of these team conflicts, you will need to communicate the new expectation and then stand your ground. Your team's first instincts will probably be to involve you initially. Transition yourself and/or your managers and supervisors out, by saying something like, "I understand that you are feeling frustrated. I need you to go have a conversation directly with X. If you need additional assistance afterward, let me know and I will be happy to help you resolve any issues."

You or another designated manager or supervisor may need to act as mediator initially, but all communication happens with interested parties in the room. Do not tolerate he said, she said. And those embroiled in the conflict must address each other in the meeting not the mediator.

Create a gossip-free zone where communication about an issue must be with the person(s) involved, period.

Provide assertive communication training if necessary. That is the gold standard for communication. It is one of the workshops I love doing with teams!

Here is a simple formula you can teach your team to use when they have a disagreement. It can be modified for any situation and, as you can see, the responsibility of finding a solution rests with the person bringing up the issue.

1. When you:_____

2. I feel:_____

3. Can you please:_____

And encourage team members to really listen to one another. Teach them to mirror back what they have heard and ask clarifying questions where they are uncertain. "What I think I hear you saying is this….. Can you clarify this one point for me?"

Communication is though. There is much room for misunderstanding. But engaging in assertive speaking and active listening will get you and your team out of the world of assumption and dealing in fact.

## Defeat the Drama with Positive Team Commitments

*"Only by binding together as a single force will we remain strong and unconquerable." ~ Chris Bradford*

When we are in positive relationships, we have positive thoughts and feelings about each other. We fill in the blanks of the unknown with positive assumptions. We give each other the benefit of the doubt. If someone does not complete a task, we say, "They must have had a very busy day," or, "It must have slipped her mind." Perhaps your team has already worked to assume the best of each other and this is not an issue. My guess, however, is that, since you are reading this book, you've had some issues in this area. Some of the relationships within the team have been compromised. Perhaps there is a lack of trust, warranted or not.

Today is a new day. It is time to help your team hit the reset button on their relationships. If you have followed the steps in this book, there is a renewed commitment to a focus on service. A new emphasis on defeating the drama. You need each one of your team members to make a commitment to the team to let past hurts and frustrations go. They must drop the old assumptions that led them to make snap judgments against specific team members or departments.

The team individually and collectively must work from a new set of assumptions and must commit to holding to them.

In one of your next team meetings, you must broach this subject. Acknowledge that you understand past feelings but that today is a new day. Ask them to work together to create a list of assumptions that they will form moving forward. In the absence of fact, these assumptions are where their mind must go.

For instance, if there is an error on a customer bill, do not assume that an employee in the billing department was intentionally working to make someone else's life at work more difficult. Instead, assume that it was an honest mistake or that there must have been a snafu in the process.

Communicating about an issue from a place of positive assumptions will alter the way your team interacts. Non-verbal communication will be positive and outcomes will be better.

Of course, if there is a true issue, and an employee is making intentional missteps to create drama, that must be handled by you as a leader.

Here are some examples of commitments generated by some of my clients' teams:

- We will assume our co-workers are doing their best.

- We commit to avoiding gossip.

- We commit to resolving our conflicts with good communication.

- We commit to treating each other with respect.

- We will assume that our teammates want to do a good job.

## Defeat the Drama by Communicating Roles

*"To collaborative team members, completing one another is more important than competing with one another." ~ John C. Maxwell*

As you bring your dynamic, fueled, focused, and fired up team members together, it will be important for each to know his or her role, and how it coordinates with others. If each individual is taking unbridled action, he or she needs to know where internal resources exist within their team. If an employee becomes a champion for a customer with an issue, he or she will need to know where to go for answers or help.

It is also important to know the boundaries; should an individual delegate a task to a co-worker or separate department or should an individual own it. When there is a hiccup in customer service, knowledge of organizational roles will help to diagnose the issue quickly. Not to place blame, mind you, but to fix the problem. Co-workers become powerful and efficient resources for great service.

## Defeat the Drama with Great Internal Customer Service

*"The way a team plays as a whole determines its success. .....If they don't play together, the club won't be worth a dime." ~ Babe Ruth*

Your team must understand the concept of internal customers. There are many instances when a co-worker is the customer of a team member. And since every action in the organization roles-up to customer service, whether directly or indirectly, each employee must see a team member as an extension of the customer.

I have worked with clients where team members fail to understand this concept. I had one organization where an external service manager was described as pushy by a fellow employee. This external service manager was routinely getting calls from customers who were trying to navigate the internal workings of the organization without success. By the time they reached out to this individual they were highly dissatisfied, to say the least. Many were ready to take their business elsewhere.

So, was this external service employee pushy? Yes, he sure was! But was he pushy to meet his own needs? No! He was attempting to take care of the needs of an already disgruntled customer. He needed a response to his requests immediately, or important customers would be gone and current and future revenue would be lost.

With a misaligned understanding, this 'pushy' employee perception was causing internal drama to the detriment of the customer.

Your organization must have a system for escalating customer issues through internal ambassadors and everyone on the team must know that every action is ultimately about great service and team success.

# Defeat the Drama with Complimentary Objectives

*"If a team is to reach its potential, each player must be willing to subordinate his personal goals to the good of the team." ~ Bud Wilkinson*

I find with many of my clients that goals set for individuals or teams are done in a vacuum and result in what I term competing objectives; goals that are mutually exclusive or will cause employees or departments to compete with each other rather than focus on customer service. And, of course, are a key source for drama within a team or organization.

For example, I once worked with a large healthcare organization with multiple clinics. The organization set specific targets for each around number of new customers seen. They did not pay attention to whether those customers were new to the organization as a whole. As a result, clinics competed with one another for customers as they fought over an existing pool rather than focusing on bringing in any new ones. The end sum was not necessarily an increase to the organization as a whole, a lot of ill will between locations and confused customers who did not understand why their primary clinic locations were being changed. A closer look at the overall impact had leaders re-calibrating the stated goals to create objectives that worked to achieve the end goal of adding more patients overall while encouraging harmonious relationships between clinics. A much better end result for customers too.

So as a team or organization you must maintain an intentional focus on creating complimentary objectives, goals that focus your entire team where it needs to be. Goals that avoid pitting one person or team against another inside the organization.

## Defeat the Drama with Team Celebration

*"A group becomes a team when each member is sure enough of himself and his contribution to praise the skills of the others." ~ Norman Shidle*

Yep, talking about it again. Even a mini-celebration is a reward. It gives your team the opportunity to acknowledge progress towards their goals and your mission. Again, it does not have to be a big party with food and hats.

Sports teams celebrate after every play, every shot; every chance they get. Grown men pat each other on the behinds (Please note: I am not suggesting that you use this form of celebration in your organization!). Celebrations do not have to be big, extravagant parties, although they can be. They can be small and easy to pull off.

You are working to build a solidified team. Celebrating is a way to bring people together. Lock your team with positive memories.

You have all been around a family that is full of dysfunction, I am sure. The entire focus of each person is to one up, be right, or tear down. It is not fun to be around, but for some reason these people stay connected. They are locked in a kind of negative force of gravity that keeps them solidified, no matter how miserable.

You want to create the exact opposite in your business. You want to create a solidified team pulled together through positive experiences, positive interactions, lifting each other up. Do not treat recognition or celebration like a limited resource that people must fight and bicker over. Make recognition, appreciation, and celebration abundant. Always authentic, but always present. You will model it and your team will follow.

*Lift them up; don't beat them up.*

When I teach this workshop, I often bring "Focus Stones" with me. To let you in on a little secret, they are just decorative rocks. However, if you attach the concept of focus to them they can work magic! I ask each participant to take one focus stone and then encourage them to take extra for any team members not in attendance. I instruct them to keep the stones handy at work. Some people leave them in a jacket pocket, others on a desk or next to their computer. I ask them to think of something to celebrate every time they see or touch the special stone. It just creates a point of focus for positive; a reminder of what is important. You can use anything. I have had clients put rubber bands around their wrists or attach the concept to their watch or a piece of jewelry. It does not matter what the object is. The goal is to have an often present reminder until you have created the new habit. You will be amazed at how transformative it can be to incorporate celebration into your work-life everyday.

## Catapult Task: Defeat the Drama with a Dynamic Team

**We have communication issues amongst team members or departments in these areas:**

**We will encourage assertive communication and active listening in these ways:**

**We waste time on mediating conflict in these ways:**

**I will use these strategies to get the team resolving their own disagreements:**

**I commit to pulling myself and other leaders out of the mediating roles:**

**We will utilize these strategies to improve communication:**

**We currently have negative assumptions about each other here:**

**Our team has developed a great new list of positive team commitments. They are:**

**We will keep team commitments front and center for the team in these ways:**

**We experience this team drama when roles are misunderstood:**

**Our customers feel the impact of uncertain roles in these ways:**

**I commit to creating clarity around roles in the organization in these ways:**

**These barriers stand in the way of providing great internal service.**

**We will use these strategies to escalate external customer issues through our team**

**We will use these strategies to focus the team on internal customer service**

**We have these competing objectives that cause drama amongst departments or individual team members**

**We will create complimentary objectives in these areas to eliminate this source of drama**

**We will include these forms of celebration in our business going forward:**

# Congratulations!

*"Happiness is not in the mere possession of money;*
*it lies in the joy of achievement, in the thrill of*
*creative effort." ~ Franklin D. Roosevelt*

Congratulations! If you have reached this point, you have achieved a lot. My hope is that you have completed all the Catapult Tasks or are on your way. Keep at it if you haven't! There is huge benefit in following through with each step.

My hope is that you are experiencing the advantages of working with a team that is fueled, focused, and fired up around your mission. That you have experienced to some degree the laser focus, tenacity, and drive required during a space shuttle takeoff in your business.

I hope that each of your employees has an improved sense of the important role they play in your business mission and customer experience, that each has the resources, knowledge, skills, and abilities to be successful. I hope that you are holding your team accountable so that there are consequences for making wrong choices and that you are benefitting from a team of rock stars. I hope that your team is 100% focused and engaged on the mission at hand and that they have harnessed and focused 100% of their mental capacity on your customers.

I hope that petty disagreements and discourse are a thing of the past and that your team is fueled, focused, and fired up!

If you are still in transition, keep at it. You are on your way. If you keep taking the methodical steps spelled out in this book it *will* happen. If you need additional motivation or some more convincing, visit my website *FocusForwardCoaching.com* and click on the testimonials page. You will see many stories from clients who were probably where you are now at one point or another.

Will every day be perfect? No. However, you will have the tenacity to work through the days that aren't with a clear focus on the prize. And as your team transforms, they will be helping you each step of the way. They will be working, effective extensions of you and your work.

Continue your important work and congratulations on the progress you have made! Take that moment to celebrate now.

If you are struggling to get through any of the steps in this book and want help contact me! This is what we do. I am passionate about helping others achieve. Drama zaps energy, steals focus and is the archenemy of success. Let's defeat the Drama! Find me at: *FocusForwardCoaching.com, (248) 973-7595 or KRoss@ FocusForwardCoaching.com*. You can also find a list of the services we provide below.

# Next Steps

On a scale of 1 to 10 how would your rate your success in moving forward and sticking to your commitments? Are you frustrated or energized? Enlightened or discouraged?

If you did not follow through on all that you know you need to, there is no value in beating yourself up. Give yourself grace, make an intentional choice to keep going and move forward. What will you do next? Plan it out. You've come to far to stop now. If you've followed through on all of the steps outlined, you still need an accountability partner to keep you on track. It is easy to slide back into old routines, especially when you are attempting to transform an entire team.

**Do you need additional support to make your vision a reality?**

Let's defeat the Drama! Find me at: *FocusForwardCoaching.com, (248) 973-7595 or KRoss@FocusForwardCoaching.com.*

## Focus Forward Coaching, LLC
## Service Descriptions:

**Individual Leadership Coaching**: Gain Self-Awareness. Learn who you are as a leader. Customized and highly-targeted action creates the necessary change to transform you into a powerful leader. Individual Coaching can be held in person at my office in Royal Oak, MI, at your location for multiple back-to-back sessions, or via phone.

**Group Coaching**: For groups of up to 8 individuals who have similar barriers or who are working towards related outcomes. Group coaching can help improve individuals but will also benefit a team. Each participant learns from the others as they experience success. Individual members hold each other accountable for weekly action steps. Group Coaching sessions can be held at my office in Royal Oak, MI or your location.

**Team Building**: Similar to group coaching, team building focuses more specifically on working effectively together and will dramatically improve the culture of your organization. Members learn to respect each other, improve communication, create better processes, decrease workplace drama and commit to working from positive assumptions about each other.

**Facilitated Conversations**: Experience a sense of calm and clarity during difficult conversations. Participants gain self-awareness about who they are in communication. This option is one of the most powerful tools in the Focus Forward Coaching belt. Targeted outcomes for these conversations are:

- Better understanding of the issues

- Commitments to each other for the future

- Increased skill in true listening and speaking

- Improved respect & understanding

These conversations are ideal for instances where there is a breakdown in communication.

**Culture Correction**: We will create a comprehensive, customized plan that meets your company's individual needs and catapults you towards the end goal of designing a drama free work zone. You and your staff can enjoy working in a high-energy, productive environment where full focus is on your customers. Spend more time in your area of gifting and less on staff drama, problem-solving and cleanup. Experience joy, celebrate often and achieve!

**Workshops / Speaking Engagements**: Education, self-awareness and implementation. Participants leave with individualized strategies that they can implement immediately to create positive change.

# About the Author

Kirsten E. Ross is CEO of Focus Forward Coaching, LLC, a leading coaching and culture correction firm. Her education and experience includes a Master's Degree in Human Resource Management, Senior Human Resource Certification, the Coach Training Alliance curriculum and more than 20 years of hands-on Human Resource experience working with leaders and teams.

She brings a unique blend of energy, insight and compassion to her work with clients. She will help you transform your leadership, generate dynamic teams, enhanced customer loyalty, and skyrocketing success; Defeat the Drama!

Kirsten is also the author of the book *"From People Problems to Productivity"* and has been featured as an expert for media such as: **NBC Nightly News**, **Fox 2 News**, **National Public Radio** and for publications such as **Entrepreneur Magazine**, *Working Mother Magazine* and *Fitness Magazine*.

Kirsten is an experienced speaker who adds inspiration and fun to her events, infusing humor, real life stories and self-awareness activities that keep audiences engaged. Participants leave with individualized strategies that can be implemented immediately to create positive change and defeat the drama in both their work and lives.

# Speaking Topics:

Kirsten is delighted to offer you a speaking service and support you in the design of your event. Each speaking topic will be specifically tailored to your needs and in the context of the event you are planning.

- Designing a Drama Free Workplace: Simple Strategies to Transform Your Team

- Your Culture is Your Team Machine

- Customer Loyalty: The Key to Retention & Referrals

- Do it Before the Deadline: Strategies to Achieve the Seemingly Impossible

- Assertive Communication: Your Key to Personal Power

- Behavioral Based Interviewing Strategies: The Key to Team Effectiveness

- Positive Energy, Positive Communication: The Keys to Creating a Dynamic Team

Contact her to speak at your event by emailing: Kross@FocusForwardCoaching.com or calling (248) 973-7595.

# Kirsten will Help You

Defeat the Drama

Skyrocket Success

Generate "Right Hiring"

Decrease Anger & Stress

Create Dynamic Teams

Enhance Customer Loyalty

Reduce Defensiveness

Improve Communication

Contact Kirsten for personalized support or have her speak at your event or association event.

Visit Kirsten's websites or conncct with her via her social media platforms. You will find additional resources and assistance.

Website: FocusForwardCoaching.com

Membership Site: DramaFreeWork.com

Linkedin: Linkedin.com/in/kirstenross

Facebook: Facebook.com/DramaFreeWork

Twitter: @DefeatTheDrama

Youtube: Youtube.com/user/KirstenERoss

Contact Email: KRoss@FocusForwardCoaching.com

Phone: (248) 973-7595

*Visit www.FocusForwardCoaching.com to sign up for your free newsletter and to purchase the coordinating Catapult Task Workbook and forms download.*

# Appendix

## *Performance Improvement Plan*

**Definition:** A Performance Improvement (PIP) is a written agreement between an employee and his/her manager that identifies opportunities for growth and the expectations for improvement over a specified period.

**Usage:** A manager/supervisor will initiate the PIP process when a he or she can document that an employee's performance is below identified expectations.

Sources of documentation can include:

- General policies and procedures

- Disciplinary actions

- Job descriptions

- Performance evaluations

- Customer complaints

The PIP can be initiated at any time and can occur concurrently with a disciplinary action. However, the PIP is an independent process from disciplinary action. The PIP does not affect the progression of the disciplinary process and is not considered a step in that process.

**Purpose:** To give the employee opportunity to improve performance by establishing measurable criteria, that can be met over a specified period. In addition, the PIP will give the employee opportunity to discuss low performance areas and to understand expectations of the manager/supervisor.

**Format:** Schedule a meeting with the employee's manager to discuss and review the documented reasons for the plan. Regular performance assessments should be agreed upon and scheduled for the duration of the PIP. A summary sheet is completed and signed by both parties at the final meeting. A copy will be provided for the employee.

**Criteria:** Criteria are defined as the standard of performance to be met by the employee. The manager, with input from the employee, will determine the standard. All criteria should be measurable and acknowledged by both parties.

The PIP also may include: extra training courses, additional education, and counseling sessions, as deemed necessary for successful job performance.

**Accountability:** The employee is responsible for reporting to the manager when circumstances impeded his/her ability to complete the guidelines of the PIP.

# PERFORMANCE IMPROVEMENT PLAN

**Employee Name:** _____ **Title:** _____

**Supervisor's Name:** _____**Supervisor's Title:** _____

**Date Reviewed with Employee:** _____

This provides a formal Performance Improvement Plan to correct performance in areas that need improvement. To meet the expectations established for your position, you must improve in the specific area(s) noted below and continue successful performance in all other areas.

**Performance Improvement Areas:**
*(Specific areas which need improvement – use additional sheets where necessary.)*

**Performance Improvement Plan:**
*(Corrective action to be taken and dates for training, etc. – use additional sheets where necessary.)*

This is to acknowledge that I have, on the date indicated below, discussed the areas of performance in which I need to improve and the corrective action to be taken as indicated by my supervisor. My supervisor has notified me that if my work performance does not improve, it may result in progressive discipline.

My supervisor and I agree to work together to help me improve my performance to a successful level:

**Employee's Signature**: _____ **Date:** ___/__/__

**Employee Comments:**

**Supervisor's Signature**: _____ **Date:** ___/__/__

**Supervisor Comments:**

**Scheduled Date(s) for Follow-up:**

**Follow-up Documentation:**

# References

Buckingham, Marcus; <u>Go Put Your Strengths to Work</u>: Free Press; 1 edition (March 6, 2007)

Hawkins, David R.; <u>Power vs. Force: The Hidden Determinants of Human Behavior</u>: Hay House, 2002

Hickman, Craig, Smith, Tom, Connors, Roger; <u>The Oz Principle</u>: Getting Results through <u>Individual and Organizational Accountability</u>: Portfolio Trade; Rev Upd edition (May 4, 2010)

Lembert, Paul, Be Unreasonable: The Unconventional Way to Extraordinary Business Results, McGraw-Hill; 1 edition (April 25, 2007)

Loehr, Jim and Schwartz, Tony: <u>The Power of Full Engagement: Managing Energy, Not Time, Is the Key to High Performance and Personal Renewal</u>; Free Press (December 21, 2004)

Wickman, Gino. <u>Traction: Get a Grip on Your Business</u>: Gino Wickman

CPSIA information can be obtained at www.ICGtesting.com
Printed in the USA
BVOW03s1340291213

340294BV00002B/10/P